Copyright © 2021 by Matilda Saunders

All rights reserved worldwide.

No part of this book may be reproduced or transmitted in any form or by any means, electronic or mechanical, including photocopying, recording or by any information storage and retrieval system, without written permission from the publisher, except for the inclusion of brief quotations in a review.

Warning-Disclaimer

The purpose of this book is to educate and entertain. The author or publisher does not guarantee that anyone following the techniques, suggestions, tips, ideas, or strategies will become successful. The author and publisher shall have neither liability or responsibility to anyone with respect to any loss or damage caused, or alleged to be caused, directly or indirectly by the information contained in this book.

CONTENTS

CHARCOAL GRILLING 101: A GUIDE TO GETTING THAT PERFECT SEAR EVERY TIME 6
    How to start a charcoal grill 6
    What to grill on high heat 7
    What to cook on medium heat 7
    What to grill on low heat 7
    How to clean a charcoal grill 8

BEEF 9
    Asian Flank Steak 9
    Planked Bison Sliders 10
    Hoisin Grilled Rabbit 12
    Grilled Entrecôte Of Beef 14
    Steak & Egg Sandwich 16
    Seared Bison Filet 17
    Smoked Beef Short Ribs 18
    Beer Can Bbq Burgers 20
    Prime Rib Roast 21
    Jalapeño Brisket Flat 22
    Tex Mex Burger 23
    Spicy Lamb Skewers (yang Rou Chuan) 24
    Reverse Seared Ribeyes 25
    Chutney-glazed Brisket 26
    Moppin' Sauce-marinated Flank Steak Fajitas 28

SIDES 29
    Dutch Oven Baked Beans 29
    Grilled Endive Salad 30
    Potato, Squash, And Tomato Gratin 31

- Burnt End Baked Beans 32
- Wood-plank Stuffed Tomatoes 33
- Grilled Onions 34
- Grilled Lemon Garlic Zucchini 35
- Corn & Tomato Salsa 36
- Corn, Bacon & Chorizo Hash 37
- Summer Squash & Eggplant 38
- Grilled Vegetable & Couscous Salad 39
- Ratatouille 40
- Cheesy Tomato Risotto 41
- Wood-plank Loaded Mashed Potatoes 42
- Smoked Potato Salad 43

BURGERS 44
- Oahu Burger 44
- Classic American Burger 45
- Quesadilla Burger 46
- The Crowned Jewels Burger 47
- Breakfast Burger 48

POULTRY 49
- Rosemary Ranch Chicken Kebabs 49
- Green Chile Chicken Chili 50
- Open-faced Leftover Turkey Sandwich 51
- Ultimate Chicken Curry 52
- Buffa-que Wings 53
- Dry Rub Smoked Chicken Wings With Buttermilk "berliner Weisse" Ranch 55
- Bacon-wrapped Bbq Quail 57
- Bacon Wrapped Jalapeño Stuffed Chicken Thighs 58
- Lemon Pepper Wings 59
- Cuban Chicken Bombs 60

Chicken Keema Burgers 61

Rotisserie Chicken 62

Barbecue Chicken With Alabama White Sauce 63

Stuffed Caprese Chicken Sandwich 65

Savory Beer Can Chicken 66

PORK 67

Maple Brined Pork Chops 67

Ham & Cheese Panini 68

Smoked Ham On Grill 69

Pork Curry 70

Baby Back Ribs With Guava Barbecue Sauce 72

Dr. Bbq's Spare Rib Surprise 74

Turkey Bacon Dogs 76

Pork Tortas Ahogada 77

Sunday Dinner Pork Roast 79

Sriracha Pork Chops 80

Smoked Porchetta On The Grill 81

Dr. Bbq's All Aces Baby Back Ribs 82

Skewered Balinese Chicken 83

Perfect Ribs 84

Beer Brined Loin Chops 85

FISH AND SEAFOOD 86

Tuna Kabobs 86

Justin Moore's Bbq Shrimp 87

Scallops With Pea-sto 88

Sesame Prawns 89

Grill-roasted Arctic Char 90

Seafood & Smoked Gouda Pasta 92

Thai Shrimp Skewers With Grilled Watermelon Salad 93

Greek Sea Bass 94

Cedar Planked Jerk Coconut Shrimp 95

Shrimp & Cheddar Tostada 96

Bacon-wrapped Stuffed Shrimp 97

Ricky Taylor's Peri Peri Lobster 98

Savory Pecan Shrimp Scampi Over Spaghetti Squash 99

Grilled Shrimp 100

Southern Catfish 101

DESSERTS 102

Best Banana Bread 102

Grilled Sopapillas 103

Grilled Fruit Pie 104

Apple Cake 106

Upside Down Triple Berry Pie 107

S'mores Pizza 108

Lemon Poppy Seed Cake 109

Seasonal Fruit Cobbler 110

Pizza Margherita 111

Peach Dutch Baby 112

Caramel Cinnamon Rolls 113

Nutella And Strawberry Pizza 114

Grilled Naan 115

Buttermilk Biscuits 116

Bread Pudding 117

RECIPES INDEX 118

CHARCOAL GRILLING 101: A GUIDE TO GETTING THAT PERFECT SEAR EVERY TIME

There's nothing like smell of a charcoal grill being fired up to get us salivating and ready to celebrate summer — but charcoal grilling can be intimidating. How do you start it? Where's the best spot for the food? When do you open the vents? Well, no need to worry — we've got you covered on the basics of grilling with charcoal.

How to start a charcoal grill

Traditional briquettes are inexpensive, light easily and burn long and steady. If you want a more intense, smoky flavor, go with hardwood charcoal (aka lump charcoal). These are blazingly hot but burn out faster.

Before you even light your grill, make sure to open to vents. The fire will need oxygen to keep going. After the charcoals are placed in the barbecue, you can control the internal cooking temperature by adjusting the vents: wider vents means hotter flames and more oxygen, while smaller vents means a cooler cooking temperature. Never close them all the way or the flames will go out.

Start your grill with a charcoal chimney; this is the easiest way to get your charcoal going. You do not need lighter fluid.

Stuff newspaper loosely in the bottom of the chimney (there is a space for it under the wire rack), then fill the chimney with charcoal. Remove top grate from grill, place chimney inside, and light the newspaper.

But how long should you let the coals burn? Let the charcoal or briquettes burn until they're covered with white-gray ash (it takes about 5 to 10 minutes for the coals to get to high heat and 25 to 30 minutes to get to medium heat).

Take the top grate of your grill off and, wearing protective grill gloves, hold the chimney by its handles and pour charcoal into the grill. Then take a paper towel soaked in vegetable oil, and spread it over grate with tongs. This is the trick to keep food from sticking to the grill.

What to grill on high heat

It takes about 5 to 10 minutes for the coals to get to high heat (about 700 degrees). Steaks, burgers and dense vegetables like corn on the cob and onions can handle high heat.

Grilling on high heat is the best way to get that perfect sear on the outside while keeping the inside juicy. To increase the temperature, open the vents to let in more oxygen. To decrease the temperature, close the vents — but not completely, or the fire will go out.

When grilling on high heat, create a two-fire zone: Stack more coals on one side of the grill for higher-temperature cooking, and the other side of the grill should have less charcoal for lower-temperature cooking. When grilling, sear foods on hot zone, then move over to cooler zone to cook through without burning.

After grilling, let the meat rest for five minutes on a cutting board. A board with a groove running around the perimeter is the perfect board since it collects all the juices the steak releases.

What to cook on medium heat

It takes about 25 to 30 minutes to get to grill to medium-heat temperature (about 500 degrees). Proteins that need to be thoroughly cooked through like pork chops, chicken, fish, uncooked hot dogs and sausages, along with denser fruits and vegetables like pineapple and eggplant, should be cooked on medium-heat.

Lots of medium-heat proteins use marinades (they will burn off on high heat). Marinate foods in a zip-top bag overnight — it fits easily in the fridge and fully envelops the meat. If you are short on time (you can't do it overnight), increase the amount of salt (things like soy sauce) and acid (things like citrus) to more quickly penetrate the meat, cutting down on time significantly.

What to grill on low heat

Christopher Arturo, Culinary Arts chef-instructor at the Institute of Culinary Education, does not recommend grilling at low heat (about 300 degrees) on a charcoal grill for the whole time because the protein will likely dry out. That being said, there are certain foods that do well cooked on high heat and then transferred to an area of the grill at low heat. Folks can do this with larger pieces of protein, like pork chops, as well as fattier fishes like salmon. Arturo also loves grilling a whole onion with this method.

How to clean a charcoal grill

Clean the grill right after cooking, while it's still hot, using a stiff-wire grill brush. Use it every time you grill to remove food particles from the cooking surface.

If you're looking for an alternative to using wire brushes (that may leave small wires and bits of metal behind), rub your grill grates with a peeled half onion," pitmaster Megan Day told TODAY Food. "Allow the grill to heat up to a high temperature. Pierce the half onion with a fork and rub the cut-side down along the grill grates. The onion's juices will release and produce steam to remove the bits and charred on debris."

BEEF

Asian Flank Steak

Servings: 4
Cooking Time: 14 Minutes

Ingredients:
- 1 (1 1/2 –pound) flank steak
- 1 recipe Spicy Thai Marinade

Directions:
1. Pour marinade into a large zip top bag and place steak inside. Refrigerate at least 30 minutes or up to overnight.
2. Remove the meat from the fridge while you preheat the grill to 500°F using direct heat with a cast iron grate installed.
3. Grilling:
4. Place flank steak on the grid and close the dome for 3 minutes.
5. Flip the steak over and cook an additional 2 minutes.
6. Close all of the vents and let the steak sit for 5 minutes or until the internal temperature reaches 130°F.
7. Remove the steak and allow it to rest for 10 minutes before slicing thinly on the bias.

Planked Bison Sliders

Servings:8
Cooking Time: 18 Minutes

Ingredients:
- 1 3⁄4 lb (790 g) bison sirloin
- 1⁄4 lb (115 g) beef fat
- 2 cups (500 mL) caraway Gouda, grated
- 12 small rustic rolls
- 1 cup (250 mL) fresh or frozen blackberries
- 1 ripe pear
- 1⁄4 cup (60 mL) honey
- 1 oz (30 mL) Jim Beam
- 1 spring fresh sage
- Salt and freshly ground black pepper to taste

Directions:

1. To prepare the meat, unwrap the bison sirloin or roast and pat it dry with paper towels. Place bison on a cooling rack over a cookie sheet. Refrigerate for at least 4-6 hours (or even overnight) to allow the meat to air dry. This reduces the moisture in your ground meat and allows for a burger that is not too wet and sloppy; they tend to fall apart.
2. Set up your meat grinder according to the manufacturer's instructions. Cut the bison sirloin into 1-2- inch (5-10cm) chunks. Chop up the beef fat. Grind the bison meat and the beef fat together. When all the meat has been ground once, give it a quick stir or mix and then grind it again. Place ground meat back into the refrigerator and allow it to rest.
3. To make the Blackberry Whiskey Compote, combine blackberries, pear, honey and whiskey in a small saucepot. Add in the sprig of fresh sage and a grind or two from your pepper mill. Heat over medium to medium-low heat, stirring occasionally, until the mixture reaches a low boil. Simmer for 10-15 minutes, stirring occasionally, until the mixture is slightly thick. Remove from heat, remove and discard spring of sage and season to taste with a little salt. Set aside.
4. Preheat the grill to 400°F using direct heat with a cast iron grate installed. Remove grilling plank from water and pat dry with paper towels.
5. Remove bison from refrigerator. Season the meat liberally with a little salt and black pepper. Scoop the meat (approx. 3 oz/85g) and firmly but gently pack the ground meat into the scoop. Unmold the little ball of meat and place on grilling plank, flat side down. Repeat with all meat. You should be able to get about 12 small balls onto each plank. Squish 'em a little if you must or grab a second plank. Never buy just one, always have a backup!
6. Place plank onto hot grill. Close dome and let bison balls plank cook for about 15-18 minutes, until the burgers are cooked to an internal temperature of 145°F/63°C, medium doneness. You don't want to overcook these burgers as they will get dry and tough. They are much better moist and juicy. Just before the burgers are done, sprinkle the caraway Gouda cheese evenly over top of them. Close dome for a minute or so until the cheese is melted.
7. Warm the rolls, then take one and tear it open. Spoon in a little Blackberry Whiskey Compote and add a burger. Repeat and serve immediately.

Hoisin Grilled Rabbit

Servings: 8
Cooking Time: 25 Minutes

Ingredients:
- 2 rabbits, about 4lb (1.8kg) in total, quartered
- 1/4 cup hoisin sauce
- for the brine
- 2/3 cup kosher salt
- 2/3 cup packed light brown sugar
- 4 tbsp pickling spice
- 8 cups hot water
- 2 tbsp Chinese five-spice powder
- for the pickled carrots
- 1/4 cup sugar
- 1/2 cup rice vinegar
- 1/2 cup water
- 2 tbsp hot sauce
- 2lb (1kg) carrots, peeled
- for the succotash
- 1 red bell pepper, left whole
- 2 ears of corn, shucked
- 2 tbsp extra virgin olive oil
- 1 cup diced red onion
- 1 large garlic clove, minced
- 1 cup fresh edamame, shelled
- kosher salt and freshly ground black pepper
- 1 tbsp thinly sliced fresh basil

Directions:

1. To make the brine, in a large bowl, whisk together salt, brown sugar, pickling spice, and water until salt and sugar have dissolved. Add ice cubes a few at a time until the liquid is no longer hot. Stir in Chinese five-spice powder. Place rabbit pieces in a large resealable plastic bag and add brine to fully cover. (Any extra brine can be refrigerated and saved for a later use.) Refrigerate for 1 hour.
2. Preheat the grill to 325°F (163°C) using direct heat with a cast iron grate installed. Place carrots, pepper, and corn on the grate, close the lid, and grill until beginning to soften and char, about 6 to 8 minutes. Remove the vegetables from the grill, place a dutch oven on the grate to heat, and close the lid. Once the vegetables are cool enough to handle, cut the kernels from the cobs, seed and dice pepper, and slice carrots into rounds.
3. To make the pickled carrots, in a small saucepan, combine sugar, vinegar, and water. Place on the stovetop over high heat and bring to a boil. Reduce heat to low and stir in the hot sauce. Remove from the heat. Pack the sliced carrots into several airtight containers and pour the hot pickling solution over the carrots to cover. Cover the containers with lids, let cool to room temperature, and refrigerate for at least 2 hours before using. (Pickled carrots can be made in advance and will keep for up to 6 months in the fridge.)
4. Remove rabbit from the brine and pat dry with paper towels. Lightly brush with hoisin sauce and place on the grate next to the dutch oven. To the dutch oven, add oil, onion, garlic, edamame, and grilled pepper and corn. Leave the dutch oven uncovered, close the grill lid, and grill rabbit until the meat reaches an internal temperature of 160°F (71°C) and the onions are soft, about 10 to 15 minutes, turning the rabbit pieces once. Season the succotash with salt and pepper to taste and sprinkle with basil.
5. Remove rabbit and the dutch oven from the grill and serve immediately with the pickled carrots.

Grilled Entrecôte Of Beef

Servings: 4
Cooking Time: 20 Minutes

Ingredients:
- Guacamole
- Spice Rub and Entrecote
- Cheesy Tortillas
- 2 Ripe Avocados
- 1 Red Onion, Finely Chopped
- 2 Tomatoes, Inside Removed, then Cubed
- 1/2 Cup (120 ml) Cilantro, Roughly Chopped
- 1 Lemon, Zest and Juice
- 4 Ribeye Steaks
- 2 tbsp (30g) Coarse Salt
- 1 1/2 tbsp (20g) Surgar
- 2 tbsp (15g) Coriander Powder
- 2 tbsp (15g) Paprika
- 2 tbsp (5g) Garlic Flakes
- 1/2 tbsp (5g) Peppercorns
- 2 tbsp (5g) Onion Powder
- 2 tbsp (5g) Fresh Thyme
- 4 Tortillas
- 1/2 Cup (60g) Cheddar Cheese, Grated
- 1/3 Cup (80 ml) Parsley, Roughly Chopped
- Cayenne Pepper
- Lemon Zest

Directions:
1. Preheat the grill to 750°F using direct heat with a cast iron grate installed. Place the steaks on the grill and cook to the desired temperature. While the meat is resting before carving, lower the temperature to 400°F and place the tortillas on the grill, allowing the cheese to melt and the tortillas to get a crust. Cut the tortillas into quarters and serve with the guacamole.
2. Mesh the avocado to desired texture with a fork. Add the rest of the ingredients and mix well. Season to taste.
3. Place all rub ingredients in a mortar and pestle or spice grinder, and grind to just before it becomes fine. Rub generously over the steaks and refrigerate for an hour.
4. Mix all the ingredients and spread evenly over tortillas. Cover with the remaining tortillas and lightly press down. Be careful before braaing as the cheese may fall out.

Steak & Egg Sandwich

Servings: 4
Cooking Time: 6 Minutes

Ingredients:
- ¼ cup sour cream
- 1 tablespoon prepared horseradish
- 1 tablespoon minced fresh chives
- ¼ teaspoon kosher salt
- ¼ teaspoons freshly ground black pepper
- 4 tablespoons plus 2 tablespoons unsalted butter
- 4 English muffins cut in half
- 4 slices beefsteak tomato, ¼ inch thick
- 4 (4-ounce) beef tenderloin steaks
- Kosher salt and freshly ground black pepper
- 4 large eggs
- 4 slices white Cheddar cheese

Directions:
1. Preheat the grill to 400°F using direct heat with a cast iron grate installed.
2. To make the horseradish cream, whisk the sour cream, horseradish, chives, salt, and pepper in a small bowl until blended. Set aside.
3. Melt 4 tablespoons of the utter in a small saucepan on the stovetop over low heat. Using a pastry brush, spread the muffin halves with butter. Place the muffin halves on the Griddle, cut side down, until toasted and lightly browned. Using a long-handled spatula, transfer the muffins to a platter. Spread each of 4 muffin halves with 2 teaspoons of the horseradish cream. Set aside.
4. Brush all the tomato slices first and then the steaks with butter, and season with salt and pepper. Place the steaks on the Grid and, while they are cooking, melt the remaining 2 tablespoons of butter on the Griddle. Crack the eggs onto the hot Griddle. Close the lid of the kamado grill and cook for 3 minutes, or until the whites of the eggs are set. Using a long-handled spatula, turn the steaks and eggs over and top each egg with a slice of cheese. Close the lid of the kamado grill and continue to cook for 2 minutes or until the cheese is melted. Using a long-handled spatula, remove each steak and place it on the bottom half of an English muffin. Top each steak with 1 egg, a slice of tomato, and the top of the English muffin. Place the assembled sandwiches on the Grid.
5. Close the lid of the kamado grill and heat for 1 minute, until the sandwiches are hot.
6. Transfer the sandwiches to a platter and serve immediately.

Seared Bison Filet

Servings:6
Cooking Time: 10 Minutes

Ingredients:
- 8 oz bison filet
- 1 tsp salt
- 1 tsp pepper

Directions:
1. Preheat the grill to 500°F using direct heat with a cast iron grate installed with grillspander platesetter Basket in place for raised direct cooking.
2. Bring the bison to room temperature and season with salt and pepper. Place the filet on the cooking grid and grill for 5 minutes per side. Remove from the kamado grill when the internal temperature reaches 125°F.
3. Let rest 5 minutes before slicing and serving.

Smoked Beef Short Ribs

Servings: 4
Cooking Time: 250 Minutes

Ingredients:
- 1 teaspoon garlic powder
- 1 teaspoon onion powder
- 1 teaspoon smoked Spanish paprika
- ½ teaspoon cayenne pepper
- ½ teaspoon dried thyme
- 4 pounds bone-in beef short ribs, cut 2 to 2½ inches thick
- 16 ounces lager beer
- 2 cups chicken stock
- 2 cups white balsamic vinegar
- 4 tablespoons salted butter, cubed
- 1 teaspoon garlic powder
- 1 teaspoon onion powder
- 1 teaspoon smoked Spanish paprika
- ½ teaspoon cayenne pepper
- ½ teaspoon dried thyme
- ½ teaspoon ground coriander
- 1 tablespoon kosher salt

Directions:
1. Preheat the grill to 225°F using direct heat with a cast iron grate installed.
2. Generously rub the short ribs with the spices.
3. Place the hickory chips in a small bowl, cover with water and let soak for at least 1 hour. Drain and scatter over the preheated charcoal. Using barbecue mitts, place the grid in the grill.
4. Place the ribs on the grid; close the dome of the grill. Let the ribs smoke 1½ to 2 hours. Once the short ribs have finished smoking, transfer the ribs to the baking dish.
5. Using the Grill Gripper and barbecue mitts, carefully remove the grid and add the platesetter and replace the grid. Raise the internal temperature of the kamado grill to 375ºF.
6. Mix the beer and the chicken broth in a large bowl and set aside. Place the vinegar in a heavy-bottomed saucepan on the stove top over medium heat for about 15 minutes, or until the liquid has reduced by half.
7. Pour the beef and chicken mixture over the ribs.
8. Cover the dish tightly with aluminum foil; place in the preheated kamado grill for 2½ hours, or until the ribs are fork tender.
9. Warm the reduced vinegar over low heat. Using a whisk, add the butter a little at a time, stirring constantly, until the butter is emulsified. Do not boil. Transfer the ribs to plates, top with the sauce and serve immediately.
10. Mix the garlic powder, onion powder, paprika, cayenne pepper, thyme, coriander and salt in a small bowl.

Beer Can Bbq Burgers

Servings: 4
Cooking Time: 30 Minutes

Ingredients:
- 1/2 medium white onion
- 2lb (1kg) ground chuck
- 1/4 cup cooked wild rice
- 3 tbsp sweet paprika
- 2 tbsp Dijon mustard
- 2 tbsp minced garlic
- 2 tbsp kosher salt, plus more as needed
- 2 tbsp ground black pepper, plus more as needed
- 9 tbsp smoky BBQ sauce, divided
- 4 tbsp sweet pepper relish
- 4 tbsp prepared horseradish
- 4 hamburger buns
- to serve
- lettuce leaves
- tomato slices
- onion slices

Directions:
1. Preheat the grill to 400 °F (163°C) using indirect heat with a cast iron grate installed. Place onion on the grate, close the lid, and grill until beginning to soften and char, about 7 to 10 minutes. Remove onion from the grill and dice. Set aside.
2. In a large bowl, use your hands to combine beef, cooked rice, paprika, mustard, garlic, salt, pepper, and 1 tbsp BBQ sauce. Form the mixture into 4 patties, and press a can of beer or soda into the middle of each patty to create an indentation. Season the patties with salt and pepper, and fill the indentations with the grilled onion and relish, evenly dividing the filling ingredients among the 4 patties. Top each burger with 1 tbsp BBQ sauce.
3. Place the patties on the grate, close the lid, and grill until the internal temperature reaches 155°F (68°C), about 8 to 12 minutes. Don't move or flip the burgers.
4. In a small bowl, combine horseradish and remaining 4 tbsp BBQ sauce. Remove the burgers from the grill and let rest for a few minutes. While the burgers rest, place the bun halves cut side down on the grate and toast for 3 to 5 minutes.
5. Spread the bottom buns with the BBQ horseradish mixture. Place a patty on each bottom bun, top with lettuce, tomato, and onion, and place the top buns. Serve immediately.

Prime Rib Roast

Servings: 8
Cooking Time: 300 Minutes

Ingredients:
- 1 14-pound rib roast
- 1/4 cup English Pub Rub

Directions:
1. Remove from fridge and allow the roast to come to room temperature, about 30 minutes.
2. Dry the roast with paper towels and season liberally with English Pub Rub.
3. Smoking:
4. Preheat the grill to 425°F using direct heat with a cast iron grate installed.
5. Place the roast directly on the grid and close the dome.
6. Cook for 20 minutes per pound, or until the internal temperature reaches 130°F (for medium).
7. Remove from the grill and allow the roast to rest for 30 minutes before carving.

Jalapeño Brisket Flat

Servings: 6
Cooking Time: 300 Minutes

Ingredients:
- 5 lb. brisket flat, with ½ inch fat cap left on
- 2 tbsp olive oil
- Ancho Chili & Coffee Seasoning
- 1 jar sliced jalapeños

Directions:
1. Preheat the grill to 300°F using direct heat with a cast iron grate installed.
2. Rub the brisket all over with the oil, then season it liberally on all of the exposed meat using Ancho Chili & Coffee Seasoning. Let rest for 15 minutes so the rub will adhere.
3. Place the brisket on the kamado grill fat side down and cook for 3 hours. After the brisket has cooked for 3 hours, place it in the pan, fat side down. Pour the jar of jalapenos over the brisket, juice and all, then place the pan back in the grill. Cook for 1 hour. Flip the brisket over and cover the pan tightly with aluminum foil. Cook for about 2 more hours until the brisket reaches an internal temperature of 205°F and is fork tender.
4. Remove the pan from the kamado grill and let rest for 15 minutes. Slice the brisket thinly against the grain and serve.

Tex Mex Burger

Servings: 4
Cooking Time: 8 Minutes

Ingredients:
- 4 Nature's Own 100% Whole Wheat Sandwich Rolls 2 teaspoons fresh lime juice
- 1 teaspoon ground cumin
- 1 teaspoon chili powder
- 1/4 teaspoon salt
- 1/8 teaspoon black pepper
- Dash cayenne pepper
- 1 pound lean ground beef
- 4 slices Manchego, Chihuahua or Cheddar cheese 4 tablespoons sour cream
- Jalapeño pepper jelly

Directions:
1. Preheat the grill to 350°F using direct heat with a cast iron grate installed.
2. Combine lime juice, cumin, chili powder, salt, black pepper and cayenne pepper in a large bowl; mix well. Add beef; mix well. Form into 4 patties.
3. Cook about 4 minutes per side, adding cheese slices during the last 2 minutes of grilling.
4. Toast insides of sandwich rolls. Spread 1 tablespoon sour cream on each roll. Place burgers on roll bottoms. Garnish with jelly.

Spicy Lamb Skewers (yang Rou Chuan)

Servings: 6
Cooking Time: 26 Minutes

Ingredients:
- 1 lamb roast (2 pounds)
- 6 to 8 skewers
- 3 tablespoons cumin seeds
- 1 tablespoon black peppercorns
- 1 tablespoon dried chili flakes
- 1 tablespoon salt
- 1 ½ teaspoons onion powder
- ½ teaspoon garlic powder

Directions:
1. In a small skillet, toast the cumin seeds and peppercorns for 1 to 2 minutes. Move the seeds around in the pan for even toasting. Once they become fragrant, remove from the heat. Place into a spice or coffee grinder on medium setting. Pulverize the seeds. Dump out into a small bowl and add the remaining ingredients for the spice rub. Set aside.
2. Cut the lamb roast into 1¼-inch cubes. Place the lamb cubes into a large bowl. Pour the spice rub into the bowl and toss to coat all of the meat. Set aside for 15 minutes.
3. Preheat the grill to 450°F using direct heat with a cast iron grate installed.
4. When the temperature is steady, oil the grill grates right before putting on the kebabs. Using long-handled tongs, dip some folded paper towels in a high smoke point cooking oil and wipe down the grill grates, making at least three good passes to create a nonstick surface.
5. Thread the lamb cubes onto the skewers, about 6 to 8 pieces per skewer. Place the kebabs onto the grill. Cook for 10 to 12 minutes, turning every few minutes. Remove the kebabs from the grill and serve. We recommend an ice cold beer to accompany these delicious kebabs.

Reverse Seared Ribeyes

Servings: 4
Cooking Time: 5 Minutes

Ingredients:
- 2 ribeye steaks, at least 2 inches thick
- Classic Steakhouse Seasoning
- Roasted Garlic, Basil & Parsley Banner Butter

Directions:
1. Preheat the grill to 250°F using direct heat with a cast iron grate installed.
2. Bring the ribeyes to room temperature and season all sides liberally with Classic Steakhouse Seasoning. Connect the kamado grill Genius for 250°F kamado grill temperature and 125°F meat temperature. Remove the steak when the internal temperature reaches 125°F. Disconnect the kamado grill Genius.
3. Set the kamado grill for direct cooking without a platesetter at 550°F.
4. Sear each side of the steak for 1 minute. Remove the steak from the kamado grill when the internal temperature reaches 135°F. Smear the steak with herb butter (we used Roasted Garlic, Basil & Parsley Banner Butter) and let rest for 10 minutes. Slice and enjoy!

Chutney-glazed Brisket

Servings: 8
Cooking Time: 300 Minutes

Ingredients:
- 1 ½ cups mango chutney
- 1 cup apple cider vinegar
- 1 cup tomato sauce
- ½ cup ketchup
- ½ cup firmly packed brown sugar
- 1 tablespoon Worcestershire sauce
- 1 (6-pound) beef brisket
- 2 cups white vinegar
- ¾ cup Tricolor Pepper Rub
- 2 cups Beer Mop
- 2 tablespoons freshly ground tri-colored peppercorns (black, white, and pink)
- 2 tablespoons sweet paprika
- 2 tablespoons garlic powder
- 2 tablespoons onion powder
- 2 tablespoons kosher salt
- 2 tablespoons dried oregano
- 1 tablespoon chili powder
- 1 teaspoon celery seed
- 2 tablespoons light brown sugar
- 1 cup white vinegar
- 1 cup beer
- ½ cup sliced red onion
- 2 cloves garlic, minced
- 1 tablespoon kosher salt

Directions:
1. Preheat the grill to 225°F using direct heat with a cast iron grate installed.
2. Mix the chutney, apple cider vinegar, tomato sauce, ketchup, brown sugar, and Worcestershire sauce in a medium bowl, until all the ingredients are combined, and set aside. Place the brisket in a large bowl, pour the white vinegar over the brisket, and let the brisket sit for 5 minutes. Transfer the brisket to a rimmed sheet pan and season all over with the pepper rub.
3. Place the brisket on the grid and close the lid of the grill. Cook for 30 minutes, mopping with the beer mop at 15 minutes. Turn the brisket over and close the lid of the grill. Mopping every 15 minutes, cook for another 30 minutes, or until the brisket is brown. Transfer the brisket to a rimmed sheet pan lined with aluminum foil.
4. Using the Grill Gripper and barbecue mitts, carefully remove the grid and add the platesetter.
5. Pour the chutney mixture over the brisket, wrap with the foil, and seal tightly. Place the brisket on the cooking grid and close the lid of the grill. Continue to cook for 4 hours, or until the brisket is very tender. Transfer the brisket to a rimmed sheet pan and let rest for 10 minutes, still in the foil.
6. Remove the foil, slice the brisket against the grain, and place on a platter. Serve immediately.
7. Peppercorns come from berries that grow in clusters on vines. The berries are dried and sold either whole or ground. The most common and recognized peppercorns are black; however, tri-colored peppercorns, which can be found in the spice section of most grocery stores, are used in this rub. If these are not available, substitute black peppercorns.
8. Place all the ingredients in a small bowl. Using a wooden spoon, stir to blend well. Store in an airtight container.
9. You can really get creative with this mop recipe. Lager (light beer) is used here, but for a more pronounced flavor try using a more robust beer. You can also change the flavor by substituting a more exotic, flavored vinegar for the white vinegar. This mop does great things for Chutney-Glazed Beef Brisket.
10. Using a whisk, combine all the ingredients in a small bowl. If not using immediately, store in an airtight container in the refrigerator for up to 1 week.

Moppin' Sauce-marinated Flank Steak Fajitas

Servings:
Cooking Time: Minutes

Ingredients:
- Flank steak (1-2 lbs)
- ½ cup   Moppin' Sauce
- Salt and pepper to taste
- 1 bell pepper, julienned
- 1 onion, julienned
- Corn or flour tortillas
- Cooking spray or 1 tbsp extra virgin olive oil

Directions:
1. Put the flank steak into a resealable bag and cover with the   Moppin' Sauce. Squeeze the air out of the bag and close it, move the meat around to make sure it is coated with sauce. Put in the refrigerator and marinate for 4 to 24 hours.
2. Preheat the grill to 400°F using direct heat with a cast iron grate installed. Add the plancha griddle for indirect cooking on half of the grillspander, leave the other half open for direct grilling.
3. Remove the steak from the marinade and season it with salt and pepper, giving it a good even coating to form a crust. Set aside.
4. Grill the onions and peppers on the plancha griddle for 7-10 minutes or until soft with some caramelized color. On the direct side, grill the flank steak to desired temperature.
5. Cut against the grain in thin slices. Built the fajitas with a tortilla, peppers and onions; top with cheese dip!

SIDES

Dutch Oven Baked Beans

Servings: 16
Cooking Time: 40 Minutes

Ingredients:
- 6 scallions, plus more to garnish
- 1lb (450g) bacon, diced
- 3 garlic cloves
- 4 x 15oz (420g) cans Great Northern beans
- 2 tbsp Chinese five-spice powder
- 1/2 cup chopped fresh cilantro
- 2 tbsp black bean garlic sauce
- 2 tsp ground ginger
- 3 tbsp soy sauce
- 1 cup sweet chili sauce

Directions:
1. Preheat the grill to 400°F (204°C) using indirect heat with a cast iron grate installed and a dutch oven on the grate. Place scallions on the grate around the dutch oven, close the grill lid, and grill until beginning to char, about 2 minutes. Chop scallions and set aside.
2. Place bacon in the dutch oven, close the grill lid, and cook until crisp, about 15 to 20 minutes, stirring occasionally. Use a slotted spoon to remove bacon from the dutch oven and set aside.
3. Drain all but 2 tbsp bacon fat from the dutch oven. Add scallions and garlic, close the grill lid, and cook until just fragrant, about 1 minute. Add beans, five-spice powder, cilantro, garlic sauce, ginger, soy sauce, and chili sauce, and stir to combine. Place the lid on the dutch oven, close the grill lid, and cook beans until heated through, about 15 minutes.
4. Remove the dutch oven from the grill, and stir bacon into the baked beans. Garnish with sliced scallions, and serve immediately.

Grilled Endive Salad

Servings: 6
Cooking Time: 2 Minutes

Ingredients:
- 2 cups frisee
- 1/2 cup pecan halves
- 1/4 cup dried cranberries
- 1/4 cup crumbled bacon
- 2 heads endive
- 1 bunch spinach, cleaned and stems removed
- 1/4 cup olive oil
- 2 Tablespoons Dijon Mustard
- 1 Tablespoon honey
- 1 shallot, finely minced
- The juice of 1 lemon
- Kosher salt and fresh cracked pepper to taste

Directions:
1. In a large bowl, combine dressing ingredients. Set aside.
2. Grilling:
3. Split endive down the middle, lengthwise and preheat the grill to 425°F using direct heat with a cast iron grate installed.
4. Remove the endive and slice into half rounds.
5. Toss shredded frisee, sliced endive, spinach, pecans, and cranberries in the dressing and serve immediately.

Potato, Squash, And Tomato Gratin

Servings: 8
Cooking Time: 35 Minutes

Ingredients:
- 1 lb Yukon gold potatoes, sliced 1/4 inch thick
- 1 lb yellow squash, sliced 1/4 inch thick
- 1/2 cup shredded parmesan cheese
- 5 tomatoes, sliced 1/4 inch thick
- 1/4 cup olive oil, divided
- 2 Tablespoons garlic, minced
- 1 tsp salt
- 1/2 tsp pepper

Directions:
1. Line the bottom of the dutch oven with 2 Tablespoon olive oil.
2. Layer potatoes on the bottom, topped with squash, and topped with tomatoes.
3. Season the tomatoes with salt, pepper, half of the garlic, and half of the parmesan cheese.
4. Repeat with remaining potatoes, squash, and tomatoes.
5. Season with salt, pepper, and remaining garlic.
6. Drizzle with remaining 2 Tablespoon of olive oil and top with remaining parmesan cheese.
7. Grilling:
8. Preheat the grill to 375°F using direct heat with a cast iron grate installed.
9. Place the dutch oven, uncovered, into the grill and close the dome for 30-35 minutes or until the potatoes are cooked through.

Burnt End Baked Beans

Servings: 6
Cooking Time: 30 Minutes

Ingredients:
- 8 oz bacon, finely diced
- 2 cups "burnt ends" from smoked brisket, finely chopped
- 1/2 cup onion, minced
- 2 cloves garlic, minced
- 1 cup favorite barbecue sauce (we like the Classic Texas Barbecue Sauce)
- 1 cup chicken broth
- 1/4 cup brown sugar
- 2 Tablespoons ketchup
- 1 Tablespoon brown mustard
- 2 (15 oz) cans pinto beans, drained and rinsed

Directions:
1. Preheat the grill to 350°F using direct heat with a cast iron grate installed with the dutch oven on the grid.
2. Add the bacon to the dutch oven and cook until crisp.
3. Add onion and garlic and cook 1 minute more.
4. Add remaining ingredients, stir to combine.
5. Cover and lower the dome for 1 hour. Serve hot.

Wood-plank Stuffed Tomatoes

Servings: 8
Cooking Time: 20 Minutes

Ingredients:
- 4 beefsteak tomatoes
- 1 cup chopped fresh flat-leaf parsley
- ¾ cup Italian-style breadcrumbs
- 1 cup grated provolone
- ¼ tsp ground black pepper
- 1 tsp unsalted butter, softened
- 2 tbsp extra virgin olive oil

Directions:
1. Place a 4 x 9in (10 x 23cm) wood plank in a baking dish, cover with cold water, and place heavy cans or stones on the plank to keep it submerged. Soak for 1 to 2 hours.
2. Preheat the grill to 425°F (218°C) using indirect heat with a standard grate installed. Place the wood plank on the grate.
3. Cut tomatoes in half horizontally and hollow out the insides, discarding the seeds and reserving the pulp. Chop the reserved pulp and place in a medium bowl. Add parsley, breadcrumbs, provolone, and pepper, and mix gently to combine. Fill each tomato half with the breadcrumb mixture and top with a drizzle of oil.
4. Flip the plank over, spread butter on the hot side, and arrange tomatoes cut side up on the plank. Place the plank on the grate, close the lid, and cook until the tops are browned and the tomatoes are soft, about 20 minutes. Remove tomatoes from the grill and serve immediately.

Grilled Onions

Servings: 4
Cooking Time: 60 Minutes

Ingredients:
- 4 large sweet onions
- 4 Tablespoons butter
- 1 tsp salt
- 1/2 tsp pepper

Directions:
1. Remove the stem end of each onion and peel the skin away.
2. With a melon baller, remove 1 inch of the core of the onion being careful not to disturb the root end.
3. Place 1 Tablespoon of butter, 1/4 tsp salt, and 1/8 tsp pepper into each onion.
4. Grilling:
5. Wrap the onions in aluminum foil and place on a 225°F grill for 1 hour with the dome closed.
6. Unwrap the onions and serve warm.

Grilled Lemon Garlic Zucchini

Servings: 6
Cooking Time: 5 Minutes

Ingredients:
- 4 zucchini, sliced lengthwise into 1/2 inch slices
- 1/4 cup butter, softened
- 2 tsp parsley, chopped
- 3 cloves garlic, minced
- The zest and juice of 1 lemon

Directions:
1. In a small dish, combine butter, parsley, garlic, lemon zest, and lemon juice.
2. Liberally brush each zucchini slice with the butter mixture.
3. Grilling:
4. Place the zucchini on a 500°F grill and close the dome for 3 minutes.
5. Flip the zucchini and recover with the dome for an additional 2 minutes.
6. Drizzle remaining butter on top of zucchini as it comes off the grill. Serve warm.

Corn & Tomato Salsa

Servings: 8
Cooking Time: 10 Minutes

Ingredients:
- 6 ears of corn, shucked
- 1 lime, halved
- 1 avocado, halved
- 1lb (450g) grape tomatoes, quartered
- 1/2 tsp kosher salt, plus more as needed
- 1/2 tsp ground black pepper, plus more as needed
- 2 tsp olive oil
- 4oz (110g) blue cheese, crumbled
- 10 fresh basil leaves, sliced

Directions:
1. Preheat the grill to 425°F (218°C) using direct heat with a cast iron grate installed. Place corn, avocado, and lime on the grate, close the lid, and grill until beginning to soften and char, about 7 to 10 minutes. Transfer the corn, avocado, and lime to a cutting board. Cut the kernels from the corn and dice the avocado.
2. In a large bowl, gently combine corn, tomatoes, avocado, salt, and pepper. Squeeze the grilled lime over top, drizzle with olive oil, and toss to coat.
3. Top the corn mixture with blue cheese and basil, and toss one final time. Season with salt and pepper to taste. Serve immediately.

Corn, Bacon & Chorizo Hash

Servings: 4
Cooking Time: 40 Minutes

Ingredients:
- 4 ears of corn, shucked
- 2 Fresno peppers
- 1lb (450g) new potatoes, halved if large
- 8oz (225g) chorizo sausage, casings removed
- 8oz (225g) thick-cut bacon, diced
- 2 shallots, finely diced
- kosher salt and freshly ground black pepper

Directions:
1. Preheat the grill to 350°F using indirect heat with a cast iron grate installed and a cast iron skillet on the grate. Place corn, peppers, and potatoes on the grate around the skillet, close the grill lid, and grill until beginning to soften and char, about 6 to 10 minutes. (Peppers and corn cook more quickly than the potatoes.) Remove the vegetables from the grill. Cut the kernels from the cobs, seed and dice the peppers, and dice the potatoes. Set aside.
2. In the hot skillet, cook chorizo for 10 minutes, stirring once or twice. Transfer the cooked chorizo to a platter and set aside. Return the skillet to the grill, add bacon, close the grill lid, and cook until crisp and the fat has rendered, about 10 minutes. Drain the bacon grease, reserving 1 tbsp in the skillet along with the cooked bacon, and return the skillet to the grill.
3. Add shallots to the skillet, close the grill lid, and sauté until soft and translucent, about 2 minutes. Add corn kernels, potatoes, and chorizo, close the grill lid, and sauté for 5 to 7 minutes more. Add half the diced peppers and season with salt and pepper. Taste to check the spice level before adding the remaining diced peppers. Stir and cook for 1 minute more. Remove the hash from the grill and serve immediately.

Summer Squash & Eggplant

Servings: 6
Cooking Time: 35 Minutes

Ingredients:
- 1 medium yellow squash
- 2 medium zucchini
- 1/4 cup olive oil
- 2 medium yellow onions, sliced into half moons
- 1 medium eggplant, peeled and cut into cubes
- 2 garlic cloves, minced
- 1/2 tsp dried oregano
- 2 cups dry white wine, such as Chardonnay
- 4 tbsp unsalted butter
- kosher salt and freshly ground black pepper
- lemon slices, to serve (optional)

Directions:
1. Preheat the grill to 425°F (218°C) using direct heat with a cast iron grate installed and a dutch oven on the grate. Place squash and zucchini on the grate around the dutch oven, close the lid, and grill until beginning to soften and char, about 5 to 7 minutes. Remove vegetables from the grill and slice into rounds.
2. In the hot dutch oven, heat oil until shimmering. Add onions, and sauté until translucent, about 7 to 8 minutes. Add squash, zucchini, eggplant, garlic, and oregano. Close the lid and sauté until vegetables begin to soften, about 15 minutes. Add white wine, close the grill lid, and simmer until the vegetables have begun to soften and the liquid has reduced by half, about 5 minutes.
3. Remove the dutch oven from the grill and add the butter, stirring until melted. Season well with salt and pepper and a squeeze of lemon. Serve hot with lemon slices (if using).

Grilled Vegetable & Couscous Salad

Servings: 6
Cooking Time: 30 Minutes

Ingredients:
- 1 small zucchini, halved
- 1 small yellow squash, halved
- 1/2 red onion
- 6 sun-dried tomatoes
- 1 tbsp olive oil
- 2 cups uncooked Israeli couscous
- 4 cups vegetable stock, heated
- 4 basil leaves, stacked, rolled, and cut crosswise into thin strips, plus more to garnish
- 2 tbsp coarsely chopped fresh flat-leaf parsley, plus more to garnish
- for the marinade
- 1/4 cup balsamic vinegar
- 1/2 tsp Dijon mustard
- 1 garlic clove, coarsely chopped
- 1/2 cup olive oil
- kosher salt and freshly ground black pepper

Directions:
1. To make the marinade, in a small bowl, whisk together vinegar, mustard, and garlic. Slowly add oil, whisking until combined. Season with salt and pepper to taste.
2. Place zucchini, yellow squash, onion, and sun-dried tomatoes in a shallow dish. Pour half the marinade over the vegetables, toss to coat, and let sit at room temperature for 15 minutes. Cover the remaining marinade and set aside.
3. Preheat the grill to 400°F (204°C) with a cast iron grate installed and a dutch oven on the grate. Remove the vegetables from the marinade and place on the grate around the dutch oven. Close the lid and grill until beginning to soften and char, about 7 to 10 minutes. Transfer the vegetables to a cutting board and cut into bite-sized pieces. Set aside.
4. In the hot dutch oven, heat oil until shimmering. Add couscous, and toast until lightly golden brown, about 2 minutes. Add vegetable stock until couscous is just covered (add hot water if more liquid is needed to cover), close the grill lid, and bring to a boil. Cook until firm to the bite, about 7 to 10 minutes, and drain well.
5. Spoon the couscous into a large serving bowl and add the grilled vegetables, basil, and parsley. Drizzle the reserved marinade over top, and toss well to coat. Serve at room temperature with more basil and parsley to garnish.

Ratatouille

Servings: 4
Cooking Time: 30 Minutes

Ingredients:
- 1/2 cup fresh, shredded basil
- 2 cloves garlic, minced
- 2 large tomatoes, chopped
- 1 red bell pepper, chopped
- 1 large eggplant, peeled and cut into 1/2 inch cubes
- 1 onion, sliced thin
- 1/4 cup olive oil
- 1/4 tsp dried oregano
- 1/4 tsp dried thyme
- 1/4 tsp fennel seeds
- 3/4 tsp salt

Directions:
1. Preheat the grill to 350°F using direct heat with a cast iron grate installed with the dutch oven on the grid.
2. Add olive oil to the pot and toast oregano, thyme, and fennel for 1 minute.
3. Add onion and cook for 5 minutes or until the onion is soft.
4. Add remaining vegetables, cover, and lower the dome for 20-25 minutes.
5. Serve topped with basil.

Cheesy Tomato Risotto

Servings: 6
Cooking Time: 35 Minutes

Ingredients:
- 1 tbsp unsalted butter
- 1/2 red onion, chopped
- 3 garlic cloves, minced
- 3/4 cup Arborio rice
- 3 cups chicken stock, warmed, plus more as needed
- 2 medium Roma tomatoes, diced small
- 2oz (55g) freshly shredded Parmesan cheese
- 2 scallions, thinly sliced
- 1 tbsp chopped fresh flat-leaf parsley

Directions:
1. Preheat the grill to 350ºF (177°C) using indirect heat with a standard grate installed and a dutch oven on the grate. In the hot dutch oven, melt butter. Add onion and garlic, close the grill lid, and cook until barely beginning to soften, about 2 minutes. Add rice, stir, and close the grill lid. Cook until rice is coated with butter and slightly toasted, about 2 to 3 minutes.
2. Add warm stock to the rice 1 cup at a time, stirring often. Add more stock only after the liquid from the previous addition is absorbed. (This will take about 10 minutes each time you add the liquid.) Add tomatoes and cheese, and stir until cheese melts. Add scallions and parsley, and stir until just combined. Remove the dutch oven from the grill and serve immediately.

Wood-plank Loaded Mashed Potatoes

Servings: 16
Cooking Time: 50 Minutes

Ingredients:
- 1lb (450g) red potatoes
- 1lb (450g) Yukon Gold potatoes
- 1 tbsp kosher salt, plus 1 tsp
- 2 strips bacon, diced
- 2 tbsp unsalted butter
- 1/4 cup sour cream
- 1/4 cup heavy cream
- 4oz (113g) shredded Cheddar cheese, plus more for topping
- 4 scallions, thinly sliced, plus more for topping
- freshly ground black pepper

Directions:
1. Place a 4 x 9in (10 x 23cm) cedar wood plank in a baking dish, cover with cold water, and place heavy cans or stones on the plank to keep it submerged. Soak for 1 to 2 hours.
2. Place red potatoes and Yukon Gold potatoes in a large stockpot and add cold water to cover by several inches. Place the pot on the stovetop over high heat, add 1 tsp salt, and bring to a boil. Reduce to a simmer, cover, and cook until potatoes are fork tender, about 25 minutes. Drain potatoes, reserving 1 cup cooking water.
3. Preheat the grill to 350°F (177°C) using direct heat with a standard grate installed and a cast iron skillet on the grate. Add bacon to the hot skillet, and cook until bacon is crisp and the fat has rendered, about 10 to 15 minutes, stirring occasionally. Transfer the cooked bacon pieces to a plate lined with a paper towel.
4. In a large bowl, combine potatoes, butter, sour cream, heavy cream, Cheddar cheese, scallions, bacon, and 1 tbsp salt. Mash with a potato masher until potatoes have broken down and cheese and sour cream are fully incorporated. If potatoes are too stiff, add some of the reserved cooking water.
5. Place the soaked plank on the grate and allow it to heat for 2 to 5 minutes, then flip it over. Scoop the mashed potatoes onto the heated side of the plank. Top the potatoes with a little Cheddar cheese, close the lid, and cook until cheese has melted and potatoes have browned slightly, about 7 to 10 minutes. Remove potatoes from the grill, sprinkle with scallions, and serve immediately.

Smoked Potato Salad

Servings: 8
Cooking Time: 120 Minutes

Ingredients:
- 4 large baking potatoes
- 4 large eggs, hard boiled and finely chopped
- 2 green onions, finely chopped
- 2 large dill pickles, finely chopped
- 1 rib celery, finely diced
- 1/2 cup mayonnaise
- The juice of 1 lemon
- 1/2 tsp black pepper
- 1/2 tsp celery seed
- 1/2 tsp dried dill

Directions:
1. Scrub the potatoes.
2. Grilling:
3. Place the potatoes alongside meat that is smoking at 225°F.
4. Assembly:
5. When the potatoes are fork tender, chill in the refrigerator for 30 minutes.
6. Peel and cut potatoes into small cubes.
7. In a large bowl, combine dressing ingredients.
8. Add potatoes, eggs, green onion, pickle, and celery to the dressing and gently toss

BURGERS

Oahu Burger

Servings: 4
Cooking Time: 12 Minutes

Ingredients:
- 2 lbs ground beef
- 1/4 cup thickened Teriyaki Marinade
- 1/4 cup mayonnaise
- 1/2 tsp sambal or sriracha
- 4 slices fresh pineapple, cored
- 4 slices tomato
- 4 slices butter lettuce
- 4 Hawaiian hamburger buns

Directions:
1. Form ground beef into four patties and season both sides with salt and pepper.
2. In a small bowl, mix mayonnaise with hot chile sauce and spread on buns.
3. Top each bun with a burger, slice of pineapple, lettuce and tomato.
4. Grilling:
5. Preheat the grill to 500°F using direct heat with a cast iron grate installed.
6. Place burgers on the grid and close the dome for 3 minutes.
7. Flip burgers, baste with Teriyaki Marinade, and place the pineapple slices on the grid. Close the dome for 2 more minutes.
8. Flip the burgers again and baste with remaining Teriyaki Marinade. Close the dome.
9. Close all of the vents and allow the burgers to sit for 5 minutes.

Classic American Burger

Servings: 4
Cooking Time: 12 Minutes

Ingredients:
- 2 lbs ground beef
- 1/2 tsp salt
- 1/4 tsp pepper
- 4 slices American cheese
- 4 hamburger buns
- Green Leaf Lettuce
- Sliced Tomato
- Ketchup
- Mustard
- Sliced Pickle

Directions:
1. Form ground beef into four patties and season both sides with salt and pepper.
2. Grilling:
3. Preheat the grill to 500°F using direct heat with a cast iron grate installed.
4. Place burgers on the grid and close the dome for 3 minutes.
5. Flip burgers and close the dome for 2 more minutes.
6. Close all of the vents and allow the burgers to sit for 5 minutes.
7. Top each burger with a slice of cheese and close the dome for 1 more minute.
8. Build burgers with lettuce, tomato, pickle, mustard, and ketchup.

Quesadilla Burger

Servings: 4
Cooking Time: 12 Minutes

Ingredients:
- 2 lbs ground beef
- 2 Tablespoons Adobo Rub
- 1 cup shredded cheddar cheese
- 4 large flour tortillas
- Sour Cream
- Guacamole
- Salsa

Directions:
1. Form ground beef into four patties and season both sides with Adobo Rub.
2. Serve each burger with sour cream, guacamole, and salsa.
3. Grilling:
4. Preheat the grill to 500°F using direct heat with a cast iron grate installed.
5. Place burgers on the grid and close the dome for 3 minutes.
6. Flip burgers and close the dome for 2 more minutes.
7. Close all of the vents and allow the burgers to sit for 5 minutes.
8. Remove burgers and place flour tortillas on the grid.
9. Top each tortilla with shredded cheese and close the dome for 1 minute until the cheese melts.
10. Place a hamburger in the center of each tortilla and begin folding the tortilla around the burger like an envelope.

The Crowned Jewels Burger

Servings: 4
Cooking Time: 12 Minutes

Ingredients:
- 2 lbs ground beef
- 1/2 tsp salt
- 1/4 tsp pepper
- 1 lb thinly sliced pastrami
- 1 cup shredded Romaine lettuce
- 1/4 cup mayonnaise
- 2 Tablespoons ketchup
- 1/8 tsp onion powder
- 4 slices Sharp Cheddar cheese
- 4 hamburger buns
- 1 tomato, sliced

Directions:
1. Form ground beef into four patties and season both sides with salt and pepper.
2. Meanwhile, mix together mayonnaise, ketchup, and onion powder. Smear on each bun.
3. Place each pastrami and cheese covered burger on the prepared buns and top with shredded lettuce and tomato.
4. Grilling:
5. Preheat the grill to 500°F using direct heat with a cast iron grate installed.
6. Place burgers on the grid and close the dome for 3 minutes.
7. Flip burgers and close the dome for 2 more minutes.
8. Close all of the vents and allow the burgers to sit for 5 minutes.
9. Top each burger with 1/4 of the pastrami and a slice of cheese and close the dome for 1 more minute.

Breakfast Burger

Servings: 4
Cooking Time: 13 Minutes

Ingredients:
- 1 1/2 lb ground beef
- 1/2 lb ground pork breakfast sausage
- 2 Tablespoon butter
- 8 strips bacon
- 4 slices sharp cheddar cheese
- 4 Brioche buns
- 4 eggs
- 4 thick slices tomato

Directions:
1. In a medium bowl, mix ground beef and sausage until just combined.
2. Form into 4 patties and refrigerate while the grill heats.
3. Melt butter in a large skillet and fry the eggs for 2 minutes on each side.
4. Grilling:
5. Preheat the grill to 400°F using direct heat with a cast iron grate installed.
6. Place bacon on a small cookie sheet and place on the grid in the grill. Cook until crispy.
7. Place the patties on the grid and close the dome for 3 minutes.
8. Flip the burgers and replace the dome for an additional 3 minutes.
9. Close all of the vents and allow the burgers to sit for an additional 5 minutes. The internal temperature of the burger should be 150°F.
10. Place cheese on top of the burgers and cover for 1 more minute.
11. Assemble the burgers by placing a burger on the bottom bun, topping with bacon, tomato, and a fried egg.

POULTRY

Rosemary Ranch Chicken Kebabs

Servings: 4
Cooking Time: 12 Minutes

Ingredients:
- ½ cup olive oil
- ½ cup ranch dressing
- 3 Tbsp Worcestershire sauce
- 1 Tbsp minced fresh rosemary
- 2 tsp salt
- 1 tsp lemon juice
- 1 tsp white vinegar
- ¼ tsp ground black pepper, or to taste
- 1 Tbsp white sugar, or to taste (optional)
- 5 skinless, boneless chicken breast halves – cut into 1 inch cubes

Directions:
1. Preheat the grill to 400°F using direct heat with a cast iron grate installed.
2. In a medium bowl, stir together the olive oil, ranch dressing, Worcestershire sauce, rosemary, salt, lemon juice, white vinegar, pepper and sugar. Let stand for 5 minutes.
3. Add the chicken to the bowl and stir to coat with the marinade. Cover and refrigerate for 30 minutes. Thread chicken onto skewers and discard marinade.
4. Lightly oil the cooking grid. Grill skewers for 8 to 12 minutes, or until the chicken is no longer pink in the center, and the juices run clear.
5. Serve with grilled corn on the cob and grilled veggie skewers.

Green Chile Chicken Chili

Servings: 8
Cooking Time: 60 Minutes

Ingredients:
- 2 lbs ground chicken
- 1 cup chopped onion
- 1 Tablespoon garlic, minced
- 1 quart chicken stock
- 2 Tablespoons olive oil
- 1 Tablespoon ground cumin
- 1 Tablespoon dried oregano
- 4 cans (14.5 ounce) Great Northern Beans, drained and rinsed
- 2 cans (4 ounce) chopped green chiles
- Salt & Pepper

Directions:
1. Preheat the grill to 500°F using direct heat with a cast iron grate installed with the dutch oven on the grid.
2. Add oil, onion, and garlic to the pot and cook until soft.
3. Add ground chicken, salt and pepper to taste, and cook until brown.
4. Add cumin and oregano and cook for 1 minute.
5. Add chicken stock and green chiles.
6. Reduce the heat in the grill to 350°F
7. Cover the dutch oven and lower the dome for 40-50 minutes. Serve hot with shredded cheese and lime wedges.

Open-faced Leftover Turkey Sandwich

Servings: 4
Cooking Time: 14 Minutes

Ingredients:
- Sourdough bread
- 3 tsp butter, separated
- Mashed potatoes
- Stuffing or dressing
- Gravy
- Roasted turkey
- Cranberry chutney or cranberry sauce
- Salt and pepper to taste
- Arugula, optional

Directions:
1. Preheat the grill to 400°F using direct heat with a cast iron grate installed.
2. Melt one tablespoon of butter in the cast iron skillet or plancha and add the mashed potatoes. Once they have a nice crust remove and set aside. Next, add the stuffing with gravy and a tablespoon of butter. Once warmed, about 5-7 minutes, remove and set aside. Lastly, add the turkey with more gravy. Once warmed, about 5-7 minutes, remove and set aside.
3. Toast the bread with a tablespoon of butter and salt and pepper. Then pile on the cranberry chutney or sauce! Next, comes the turkey. Follow it up with the mash potatoes and stuffing. Then drizzle more gravy over. Top with arugula and serve immediately.

Ultimate Chicken Curry

Servings: 4
Cooking Time: 27 Minutes

Ingredients:
- 2 tablespoons canola oil
- 1 small onion, coarsely chopped
- 4 pieces of fresh ginger (each about the size and thickness of a 25 cent coin; no need to peel the skin), coarsely chopped
- 2 teaspoons of Raghavan's Blend (page 39 of Indian Cooking Unfolded) or store-bought Madras curry powder
- ½ cup canned diced tomatoes with their juices
- ½ cup half-and-half
- 1 ½ pounds skinless, boneless chicken breasts, cut into 2-inch cubes
- 1 teaspoon coarse kosher or sea salt
- 2 tablespoons finely chopped fresh cilantro leaves and tender stems

Directions:
1. Preheat the grill to 400°F using direct heat with a cast iron grate installed.
2. Heat the oil in a Stir-fry and Paella Pan; once the oil appears to shimmer, add the onion, garlic and ginger and stir-fry until the onion is light caramel brown around the edges (4 to 5 minutes).
3. Sprinkle the spice blend into the pan and stir to mix. Let the spices roast in the onion medley until the aromas dramatically change (10 seconds). Pour in the tomatoes and stir once or twice. By adjusting the upper and lower air vents, begin to lower the heat to 300°F and simmer the chunky sauce, uncovered, stirring occasionally, until the tomato pieces soften, the excess moisture evaporates, and some of the oils in the spices start to dot the edge of the sauce (5 to 7 minutes).
4. Pour the half-and-half into the pan and scrape the bottom once or twice to release any bits of onion, garlic, and ginger, effectively deglazing the pan and releasing those flavors back into the sauce. Transfer the chunky curry to a blender. Holding the lid down, puree the curry until it is slightly curdled looking but smooth, and saffron orange-hued.
5. Return the sauce to the pan and stir in the chicken and salt. Simmer the curry with the dome closed, stirring occasionally, until the chicken, when cut with a fork or knife, is cooked through, no longer pinkish-red, and its juices run clear (12 to 15 minutes).
6. Sprinkle the cilantro on top of the chicken curry and serve.

Buffa-que Wings

Servings: 16
Cooking Time: 40 Minutes

Ingredients:
- 16 whole chicken wings (about 3-1/2 pounds)
- 1/2 cup Tabasco sauce or your favorite hot sauce
- 1/2 cup fresh lemon juice
- 1/4 cup vegetable oil
- 2 tablespoons Worcestershire sauce
- 4 cloves garlic, minced
- 2 teaspoons coarse salt (kosher or sea)
- 1 teaspoon freshly ground black pepper
- 1-1/2 cups wood chips or chunks (preferably hickory or oak), soaked for 1 hour in water to cover, then drained
- 8 tablespoons (1 stick) salted butter
- 1/2 cup Tabasco sauce or your favorite hot sauce
- 4 ounces Maytag Blue cheese
- 1 cup mayonnaise
- 1/2 cup sour cream
- 1 tablespoon distilled white vinegar
- 1/4 cup minced onion
- 1/2 teaspoon freshly ground black pepper
- Coarse salt (kosher or sea; optional)

Directions:

1. Rinse the chicken wings under cold running water and blot them dry with paper towels. Cut the tips off the wings and discard them (or leave the tips on if you don't mind munching a morsel that's mostly skin and bones.) Cut each wing into 2 pieces through the joint.
2. Make the marinade: Whisk together the hot sauce, lemon juice, oil, Worcestershire sauce, garlic, salt and pepper in a large nonreactive mixing bowl. Stir in the wing pieces and let marinate in the refrigerator, covered, for 4 to 6 hours or as along as overnight, turning the wings several times so that they marinade evenly.
3. Make the mop sauce: Just before setting up the grill, melt the butter in a small saucepan over medium heat and stir in the hot sauce.
4. Toss wood chips or chunks in the kamado grill. Preheat the grill to 350°F using direct heat with a cast iron grate installed.
5. When ready to cook, drain the marinade off the wings and discard the marinade. Brush and oil the grid. Place the wings in the center of the hot grate, over the drip pan and away from the heat, and cover the grill. Cook the wings until the skin is crisp and golden brown and the meat is cooked through, 30 to 40 minutes. During the last 10 minutes, start blasting the wings with some of the mop sauce.
6. Transfer the grilled wings to a shallow bowl or platter and pour the remaining mop sauce over them. Serve with Maytag Blue Cheese Sauce and celery for dipping and of course plenty of paper napkins and cold beer.
7. Press the blue cheese through a sieve into a nonreactive mixing bowl.
8. Whisk in the mayonnaise, sour cream, vinegar, onion, and pepper. It's unlikely you'll need salt (the cheese is quite salty already) but taste for seasoning and add a little if necessary. The blue cheese sauce will keep in the refrigerator, covered, for several days.

Dry Rub Smoked Chicken Wings With Buttermilk "berliner Weisse" Ranch

Servings:12
Cooking Time: 240 Minutes

Ingredients:
- 3 dozen Springer Mountain Farms Chicken Wings
- 3 quart water
- ¾ lb. brown sugar
- ¾ lb. kosher salt
- 10½ oz fresh ginger
- ¾ oz coriander seeds
- ¾ oz cloves
- ¾ oz white peppercorns
- ¾ oz whole allspice
- ¾ oz mustard seeds
- 1 grapefruit
- 1 lemon, cut in ¼
- 1 lime, cut in ¼
- 1 orange, cut in ¼
- 6 tbsp brown sugar
- 3 tbsp garlic powder
- 3 tbsp onion powder
- 3 tbsp celery salt
- 3 tbsp smoked paprika
- 1½ tbsp ground cumin
- 1½ tbsp salt
- 1½ tsp mustard powder
- 3 tbsp dry sage
- 3 tbsp white pepper
- 1½ tsp ground bay leaves
- 1½ tsp cayenne pepper
- 2 ¼ cup buttermilk
- ¾ cup sour cream
- 6 tablespoons beer "preferably Berliner weisse beer"
- 2¼ teaspoon apple cider vinegar
- ¾ teaspoon salt

- ¾ teaspoon black pepper
- 1 teaspoon of dry dill
- ¼ teaspoon dried parsley
- 1½ teaspoon dried oregano

Directions:

1. Remove the chicken wings from the brine and season with the Rub. Let them set for at least one hour.
2. Preheat the grill to 250°F using direct heat with a cast iron grate installed. Cook the wings for 3 to 4 hours, turning occasionally, until the internal temperature reaches 165°F or higher.
3. Served with Buttermilk "Berliner Weisse" Ranch.
4. Mix all brine ingredients with the exception of the citrus and the fresh thyme in a large pot. Bring to boil. After boiling, ice down the mixture and add the citrus and the fresh thyme. Cover the wings with the citrus brine and refrigerate overnight.
5. For the rub, mix all of the ingredients and preserve in a dry container.
6. For the ranch dressing, mix all the ingredients and let it rest in the refrigerator at least one hour before serving.

Bacon-wrapped Bbq Quail

Servings:12
Cooking Time: 24 Minutes

Ingredients:
- 12 bone in quail halves
- 3 tablespoons   Savory Pecan Seasoning
- 1 lb bacon
- 1 cup   Vidalia Onion and Sriracha Barbecue Sauce

Directions:
1. Preheat the grill to 350°F using direct heat with a cast iron grate installed.
2. Season each quail half with   Savory Pecan Seasoning; wrap each half in a slice of bacon and secure with a toothpick.
3. Grill the quail for 8 to 10 minutes per side or until the bacon is cooked through. When the quail is almost finished, brush with the sauce. Flip the quail and baste the other side. Grill for an additional 3 to 4 minutes to caramelize the glaze.

Bacon Wrapped Jalapeño Stuffed Chicken Thighs

Servings: 6
Cooking Time: 30 Minutes

Ingredients:
- 8 boneless, skinless chicken thighs
- 4 jalapeño peppers
- 8 oz cream cheese
- 16 strips of bacon
- 1 stick of butter
- All-Purpose Rub
- Sweet and Smoky seasoning
- 1 cup salt
- 1/2 cup granulated garlic
- 1/4 cup black pepper

Directions:
1. Preheat the grill to 375°F using direct heat with a cast iron grate installed. If desired, add some pecan chips for some extra smokiness.
2. Remove the thighs from the packaging and place on a cutting board designated for poultry. Trim any excess fat on the thighs and season each side with a hefty dose of Sweet and Smoky seasoning.
3. Cut the jalapeño peppers in half lengthwise and remove the seeds and veins. Fill each half with cream cheese and sprinkle a touch of all-purpose rub on top.
4. Place the stuffed jalapeño peppers cheese side down in the center of each chicken thigh and form the meat around the pepper. Next, wrap each thigh with 2 strips of bacon.
5. Place the wrapped chicken thigh in a Drip Pan, and top each piece of chicken with a pat of butter. Cook for 30 minutes, until chicken reaches an internal temperature of 165°F.
6. Remove from the kamado grill and let the chicken rest for 8-10 minutes, sprinkle more Sweet and Smoky seasoning on the chicken and spoon some of the butter sauce over the chicken.
7. Serve immediately.
8. Mix all the ingredients together and set aside.

Lemon Pepper Wings

Servings: 4
Cooking Time: 16 Minutes

Ingredients:
- Feta Dipping Sauce
- ½ cup mayonnaise
- ½ cup sour cream
- ½ cup feta cheese
- 2 teaspoons red wine vinegar
- 1 teaspoon Worcestershire sauce
- Kosher salt and freshly ground black pepper
- ¼ cup lemon zest, lemons reserved (about 6 medium lemons)
- ½ cup extra-virgin olive oil
- 2 tablespoons granulated garlic
- 1 tablespoon kosher salt
- 1 tablespoon freshly ground black pepper
- 2 pounds chicken wings

Directions:
1. Preheat the grill to 500°F using direct heat with a cast iron grate installed.
2. Mix the mayonnaise, sour cream, cheese, vinegar, and Worcestershire sauce in a small bowl. Season with salt and pepper, blend well, and refrigerate.
3. Mix the lemon zest and olive oil in a small bowl and set aside. Mix the garlic, salt, and pepper in a medium bowl. Reserve 1 tablespoon of the garlic seasoning for later use.
4. Toss the chicken with the remaining 3 tablespoons of seasoning.
5. Place the chicken on the cooking grid and baste with the olive oil mixture. Close the lid of the kamado grill. Turn the chicken wings every few minutes, basting often, closing the lid each time. Grill for 15 minutes, or until golden brown and slightly crisp. Season with the reserved garlic mixture and cook for another minute.
6. Transfer the chicken wings to a platter, squeeze the reserved lemons over the wings, and serve immediately with the dressing.

Cuban Chicken Bombs

Servings: 4
Cooking Time: 30 Minutes

Ingredients:
- 4 bone in chicken thighs
- 4 slices of ham (cut into quarters)
- 4 slices of provolone (cut into quarters)
- 2 tbsp Dijon mustard
- 12 pickle chips
- 8 slices of bacon
- Sweet & Smoky Seasoning

Directions:
1. Preheat the grill to 300°F using direct heat with a cast iron grate installed.
2. Debone the chicken thighs leaving the skin on and position the chicken thighs skin side down. Spread equal portions of the mustard on the meat side of each chicken thigh. Place an equal amount of provolone slices, ham and pickles on each chicken thigh. Roll the chicken thighs up and wrap a piece of bacon around the middle of the chicken thigh and another around the thigh lengthwise sealing the contents with bacon. Put toothpicks through the bottom of the chicken thighs to help keep contents inside while cooking. Season the top of the bacon with the Sweet & Smokey Seasoning.
3. Cook the chicken for about an hour or until the internal temperature reaches 165°F. Remove the chicken from the kamado grill and let rest before slicing and serving.

Chicken Keema Burgers

Servings: 4
Cooking Time: 12 Minutes

Ingredients:
- 2 lbs ground chicken
- 1/2 cup fresh breadcrumbs
- 1 Tablespoon olive oil
- 2 cloves garlic, finely chopped
- 1 small onion, finely chopped
- 1 egg
- 4 pieces Naan
- 2 Tablespoons Indian Spice Rub
- 1/2 cup Greek style yogurt
- 1/2 cup finely chopped, seeded, cucumber
- 2 Tablespoons chopped fresh cilantro
- 1 tsp finely chopped green onion
- 1/4 tsp ground cumin

Directions:
1. In a small bowl, combine ingredients for the raita and set aside. The raita can be made a day in advance, covered, and refrigerated.
2. In a small skillet, heat olive oil over medium and add onion and garlic. Cook until soft and translucent. Set aside to cool.
3. In a medium bowl, combine ground chicken, bread crumbs, onion mixture, egg, and Indian Spice Rub until combined. Form 4 patties and return to the fridge to chill for 10 minutes.
4. Grilling:
5. Preheat the grill to 500°F using direct heat with a cast iron grate installed.
6. Place burgers on the grid and close the dome for 3 minutes.
7. Flip burgers and close the dome for 3 more minutes.
8. Close all of the vents and allow the burgers to sit for 5-6 minutes or until the internal temperature reaches 170°F.
9. Serve burgers on naan, topped with raita.

Rotisserie Chicken

Servings: 6
Cooking Time: 90 Minutes

Ingredients:
- 1 (4-5 lb) whole chicken, gizzards and giblets removed
- 2 quarts warm water
- 1/4 cup kosher salt
- 1/4 cup brown sugar
- 2 Tablespoons whole peppercorns
- 1 lemon, halved
- 2 lbs small waxy potatoes, cut in half (we like Yukon golds)
- 1 lbs carrots, cut into 2 inch chunks
- 1/4 cup butter, softened
- 1 onion, cut into wedges
- 2 sprigs fresh thyme
- 4 whole cloves garlic

Directions:
1. Combine brine ingredients until the salt and sugar dissolve and add enough ice to bring the brine to room temperature.
2. Submerge the chicken into the brine and allow to chill in the refrigerator for a minimum of 2 hours and up to overnight.
3. Remove the chicken from the brine and pat dry.
4. In the bottom of a cold dutch oven, place the vegetables and top with the chicken, breast side up.
5. Gently lift the skin away from the meat and rub butter beneath the skin.
6. Grilling:
7. Preheat the grill to 425°F using direct heat with a cast iron grate installed.
8. Cover the dutch oven and place on the grill. Lower the dome for 1-1 1/2 hours or until the internal temperature of the meatiest part of the thigh registers 160°F
9. Remove the dutch oven from the grill and allow it to sit for an additional 10 minutes before removing the lid.
10. Remove the chicken, place the vegetables on a platter or in a bowl. Carve the chicken and serve.

Barbecue Chicken With Alabama White Sauce

Servings: 4
Cooking Time: 40 Minutes

Ingredients:
- 4 egg yolks
- ¼ cup apple cider vinegar
- ¼ cup water
- 2 tablespoons poultry seasoning
- 2 tablespoons salt
- 1 cup grapeseed oil
- 6 chicken leg/thigh pieces
- approx. 1 ½ cups Alabama white barbecue sauce
- 2 egg yolks
- ¼ cup lemon juice
- 3 tablespoons apple cider vinegar
- 2 teaspoons salt
- ½ teaspoon garlic powder
- ½ teaspoon cayenne pepper
- 2 teaspoons ground black pepper
- 1 cup grapeseed oil

Directions:

1. In a food processor fitted with a metal blade, blend the egg yolks, vinegar, water, poultry seasoning, and salt until the yolks fluff a little, about 30 seconds. With the processor running, slowly drizzle in the oil, the mixture will blend, emulsify, and resemble a thick mayonnaise. You will hear the sound change to a whop, whop; it should take about 1 minute. Spoon the marinade into a large zip-top bag, add the chicken pieces, and massage until the chicken is completely covered with the marinade. Zip the top closed, pressing out any air as you seal the bag. Set the bag in a bowl in the refrigerator overnight or for up to 24 hours.

2. Pour ¾ cup of the Alabama white barbecue sauce into a bowl to use for basting. Preheat the grill to 400°F using direct heat with a cast iron grate installed. Remove the chicken from the marinade and pat completely dry. Scrape the cooking grid clean and coat with oil. Place the chicken, skin side down, on the grid and cover with an aluminum drip pan or tent with foil. After 10 minutes, flip the chicken pieces. Cover again with the pan or foil. After 10 more minutes, baste the chicken with the sauce, flip so the skin side is down, and baste again. Cover with the pan or foil, cook for another 10 minutes, and then baste, flip, and cover again. Cook, baste, flip, and cover one last time, for a total cooking time of 40 minutes. Discard the basting sauce. Remove the chicken from the grill and rest, tented with foil or a foil pan, for 10 minutes. Serve with remaining sauce on the side.

3. In a food processor fitted with a metal blade, combine the egg yolks, lemon juice, vinegar, salt, garlic powder, cayenne, and black pepper and process until the yolks fluff a little, about 30 seconds. With the processor running, slowly drizzle in the oil; the mixture will blend and emulsify but won't be as thick as the marinade used for the barbecue chicken. You will again hear the sound change to a whop, whop; it should take about a minute.

Stuffed Caprese Chicken Sandwich

Servings: 4
Cooking Time: 14 Minutes

Ingredients:
- 2 cups balsamic vinegar
- 3 tablespoons honey
- 4 large boneless skinless chicken breasts
- salt, pepper, and garlic powder to taste
- 4 large slices tomato
- 8 small slices fresh whole milk mozzarella
- 8 large leaves fresh basil
- 4 Cobblestone Bread Co hamburger buns (Sesame Twist works great)

Directions:
1. In a small saucepan, heat the vinegar and honey over medium/high heat (375-450°F). Bring to a boil and then reduce to a simmer, stirring regularly. When it starts to thicken and has reduced by about half (approximately 10 minutes), remove from the heat and set aside.
2. Season each chicken breast with salt, pepper, and garlic powder to taste. Cut each breast lengthwise, but not all the way, forming a "pita" shape. This is where you will place the mozzarella, basil, and tomato later.
3. Place the chicken in two large ziplock bags and pour some of the balsamic reduction into each bag, reserving a small amount for garnish. Allow to marinate in the fridge for at least 30 minutes before grilling.
4. When ready to grill, spray your cooking grid with non-stick spray or brush with canola oil. Stuff each chicken with one slice tomato, 2 leaves basil, and 2 slices fresh mozzarella. Use a toothpick to seal the opening if desired, this will make flipping the chicken easier.
5. Grill the chicken over medium/high heat, approximately 450°F, for 5-7 minutes on each side or until chicken is cooked through. This will bed determined based on the thickness of the chicken you picked. When the chicken is white throughout, it's done!
6. Place chicken onto the bottom bun and drizzle with a bit more of the reserved balsamic reduction. Top with the top part of the bun. Enjoy!

Savory Beer Can Chicken

Servings: 4
Cooking Time: 30 Minutes

Ingredients:
- 1 (4 to 5-pound) chicken
- 1 (12-ounce) can beer
- ¼ cup (60 ml) mayonnaise
- 3 Tbsp (45 ml)   Savory Pecan Seasoning

Directions:
1. Preheat the grill to 350°F using direct heat with a cast iron grate installed.
2. Pour ½ of the beer into a drip pan. Place the can with the remaining beer in the center of the Folding Beer Can Chicken Roaster and snap the arms into place at the top.
3. Put the rack into the drip pan and place the chicken onto the rack. Combine the mayonnaise and the seasoning and coat the outer skin and inner cavity of the chicken with the mixture.
4. Roast the chicken until the internal temperature reaches 165°F/74°C; remove from the kamado grill and let rest for 10 minutes. Carve and serve.

PORK

Maple Brined Pork Chops

Servings: 4
Cooking Time: 14 Minutes

Ingredients:
- 4 bone-in pork chops, about 3/4 in (2 cm) thick
- 1 recipe cold Maple Brine
- 2 tbsp pure maple syrup
- 2 cups (480 ml) water, plus 2 cups (480 ml) ice water
- 1/2 cup (120 ml) pure maple syrup
- 1/4 cup (60 g) Morton's Kosher Salt
- 1 tbsp vanilla extract
- 1 tsp granulated onion
- 1 tsp black pepper
- 1/2 tsp cinnamon
- 1/4 tsp ground nutmeg

Directions:
1. Place the chops in a large heavy-duty zip-top bag. Pour the brine over them. Seal the bag, squeezing out as much air as possible. Place the bag in a pan or bowl in case of leakage and refrigerate it for 3 to 4 hours, occasionally moving the chops around within the bag.
2. Preheat the grill to 350°F using direct heat with a cast iron grate installed.
3. Remove the chops from the brine and rinse them under cold water. Dry the chops well. Place them on the kamado grill and cook them for 5 to 6 minutes, until they're golden brown. Flip them over and cook them for another 5 to 6 minutes, until they reach an internal temperature of 150°F deep in the center. Remove them to a plate and brush each chop with the maple syrup on all sides. Serve one chop to each guest.
4. In a medium saucepan over medium heat, combine the 2 cups (480 ml) water, maple syrup, salt, vanilla, granulated onion, pepper, cinnamon, and nutmeg. Mix them well. Bring the mixture to a simmer, stirring often. Cook it for 1 to 2 minutes, until the salt and syrup are dissolved. Add the ice water to a large bowl. Pour the hot brine over the ice water. With a large spoon, mix well until everything is blended. Refrigerate the brine for at least 2 hours, until well chilled. Use it immediately or keep it refrigerated for up to 1 week.

Ham & Cheese Panini

Servings: 4
Cooking Time: 10 Minutes

Ingredients:
- 8 slices Natures Own 100% whole wheat bread
- ¼ cup spicy brown mustard
- 8 slices sharp white Cheddar cheese
- 2 cups packed baby arugula
- 1 ripe Bartlett pear, cut into 20 thin slices
- ½ pound deli-sliced smoked ham
- Olive Oil

Directions:
1. Preheat the grill to 400°F using direct heat with a cast iron grate installed.
2. Spread mustard evenly over 1 side of each bread slice. Top each of 4 bread slices with 1 slice cheese and half the arugula. Add the pear and ham slices; top with remaining arugula, cheese and bread slices.
3. Press sandwiches together slightly, brush outside of sandwiches lightly with oil Cook sandwiches on the griddle, turning once, until browned and cheese melts.

Smoked Ham On Grill

Servings: 10
Cooking Time: 60 Minutes

Ingredients:
- 7-12 lb. ham, not spiral sliced
- 3 cups apple juice - water or other juice can be used
- 2 cups of apples, oranges or other fruits, cut into small pieces
- 1 cup brown sugar
- 1 tsp black pepper
- ¼ cup of bourbon
- ¼ cup of syrup
- 2 tbsp of brown mustard

Directions:
1. Preheat the grill to 275°F using direct heat with a cast iron grate installed. We recommend the apple smoking chips.
2. Fill a drip pan with the juice and fruit and place on the platesetter.
3. Score the fat portion of the ham in a checkerboard pattern, making cuts approximately 1 inch apart, and 1 inch deep.
4. Cook for approximately 1 hour for 2 lbs. of weight. During the last hour of cooking, brush ham with the glaze. Remove when the ham has reached the internal temperature of 155- 160°F.
5. Let the ham rest before serving
6. For the glaze mix all the ingredients together and let sit for 2-3 hours.

Pork Curry

Servings: 6
Cooking Time: 20 Minutes

Ingredients:
- 2 pork tenderloins, about 3lb (1.4kg) in total, trimmed, silverskin removed, and cut into 2-in (.5-cm) pieces
- 3 cups cooked white rice
- naan bread, to serve (optional)
- for the marinade
- 4 dried red chile peppers
- 1/3 cup white vinegar
- 2 tsp ground cumin
- 1 tsp ground black pepper
- 1/2 tsp cinnamon
- 3 tsp ground cardamom
- 1 tsp ground cloves
- pinch of ground nutmeg
- 1 tsp grated fresh ginger
- 5 garlic cloves, peeled
- 1/2 cup olive oil
- 2 medium yellow onions, roughly chopped
- 1 tsp sugar
- kosher salt
- for the pickled mango
- 1/2 cup apple cider vinegar
- 1 tbsp sugar
- 1/2 tsp kosher salt
- 1 cup hot water
- 1 tbsp Vindaloo curry seasoning
- 1 ripe mango, peeled and sliced

Directions:
1. To make the marinade, in a small bowl, cover peppers with vinegar and let soak for 10 minutes. Transfer peppers and vinegar to a food processor, add remaining marinade ingredients, and blend until smooth. Transfer half the marinade to a resealable plastic bag. Reserve the remaining marinade and set aside.
2. Place pork pieces in the bag with the marinade and squeeze out any excess air. Refrigerate for at least 2 hours and up to 24 hours. Before grilling, remove from the fridge and bring to room temperature.
3. To make the pickled mango, in a small bowl, whisk together vinegar, sugar, and salt until sugar and salt have dissolved. Pack mango in a small jar and pour the vinegar mixture over top to cover. Let sit at room temperature for 1 hour.
4. Preheat the grill to 425°F (218°C) using direct heat with a cast iron grate installed and a dutch oven on the grate. Remove pork pieces from the marinade and place on the grate around the dutch oven (not inside). Close the grill lid and grill until the internal temperature reaches 140°F (60°C), about 8 to 12 minutes.
5. Transfer the grilled pork pieces to the dutch oven and add the cooked rice, reserved marinade, and pickled mango. (Discard pickling liquid or refrigerate in a sealable container for future use.) Cook until warmed through, about 5 to 7 minutes, stir occasionally. Serve immediately with warm naan (if desired).

Baby Back Ribs With Guava Barbecue Sauce

Servings: 6
Cooking Time: 250 Minutes

Ingredients:
- 3 tbsp sugar
- 2 tbsp coarse salt (kosher or sea)
- 2 tbsp freshly ground black pepper
- 1 tbsp Chinese dry mustard
- 2 tsp Chinese five-spice powder
- 1 cup Chinese rice wine, sake, or rice vinegar
- 2 racks baby back ribs (4 to 5 pounds total), membranes removed
- 8 ounces guava paste, cut into ½ inch pieces
- ½ cup rice or cider vinegar
- 1/3 cup dark rum
- ¼ cup ketchup or tomato paste
- 3 tbsp fresh lime juice
- 1½ tbsp soy sauce
- 1½ tbsp Worcestershire sauce
- 1 tbsp minced fresh ginger
- 1 tbsp minced scallion white
- ½ tsp ground cinnamon
- ½ tsp ground nutmeg
- ½ tsp ground allspice
- 3 tbsp brown sugar
- Coarse salt (kosher or sea) and fresh ground black pepper to taste

Directions:

1. Preheat the grill to 275°F using direct heat with a cast iron grate installed.
2. Prepare the rub with sugar, salt, pepper, mustard and five spice powder in a bowl and mix. Sprinkle the ribs on both sides with rub, rubbing it into the meat.
3. Arrange the ribs, bone side down. After cooking for 1 hour spray the ribs with rice wine. Cook another 3 to 4 hours and spray the ribs once or twice. When ribs are cooked, the meat will have shrunk back from the ends of the bones by about 1/2-inch.
4. In the last 30 minutes, brush the ribs on both sides with some of the guava barbecue sauce. Grill until the ribs are browned and bubbling, 2 minutes per side.
5. Transfer the ribs to a large platter or cutting board, and cut the racks in half, widthwise (or into individual ribs). Serve at once with the remaining guava sauce on the side.
6. For the guava barbecue sauce, place the guava paste, vinegar, rum, ketchup or tomato paste, lime juice, soy sauce, Worcestershire sauce, ginger, scallion whites, cinnamon, nutmeg, allspice, and salt and pepper in a heavy saucepan. Add 1/4 cup water. Gently simmer the sauce over medium heat until thick and richly flavored, 10 minutes, whisking to break up the pieces of guava paste. The sauce should be thick but pourable—add water as needed. Correct the seasoning, adding salt and pepper to taste.

Dr. Bbq's Spare Rib Surprise

Servings: 4
Cooking Time: 195 Minutes

Ingredients:
- 2 slabs (about 4 lb/1.8 kg each) whole spareribs
- 1 recipe Secret Apple Juice Injection
- 1 cup (220 g) barbecue rub such as Barbecue Rub #34
- 1 1/2 cups (360 ml) apple juice
- 1/4 cup (50 g) Sugar In The Raw or other raw sugar
- 1 tbsp Morton's Kosher Salt
- 2 tbsp yellow mustard
- 2 tbsp soy sauce
- 1/2 tsp cayenne
- 1/4 cup (60 g) Morton's Kosher Salt
- 1/4 cup (50 g) packed brown sugar
- 2 tbsp paprika
- 1 tbsp chili powder
- 1 tbsp granulated onion
- 1 tsp granulated garlic
- 2 tsp black pepper
- 1/2 cup (120 ml) apple juice

Directions:
1. A half hour before you plan to cook, peel the membrane off the back of the ribs and cut the flap of meat across the bone side off. Trim any excess fat.
2. Using the Injector, inject the ribs in between the bones from both ends until all of the injection liquid has been used up. Season the ribs liberally on both sides with the rub. Refrigerate them until needed.
3. Preheat the grill to 275°F using direct heat with a cast iron grate installed. Place the ribs meaty-side up on the kamado grill and close the dome. Cook them for 2 hours. Flip the ribs over and cook them for another hour.
4. Lay out two large double-thick sheets of heavy-duty aluminum foil. Lay a slab of ribs on each, meaty-side up. As you begin to fold the foil up around the ribs, add 1/4 cup (60 ml) of the apple juice to the bottom of each package. Continue folding the foil up around the ribs, closing it into a package. Return the rib packets to the kamado grill for 1 hour, or until the ribs are tender when poked with a toothpick.
5. Remove the ribs from the foil and place them back on the kamado grill meaty-side up. Cook them for 15 minutes more, until the ribs are firmed up. Place the ribs meaty-side down on a cutting board and use a sharp knife to cut through the slab completely at each rib. To serve, flip the ribs over, reconstructing the slabs on a platter.
6. In a medium bowl, combine the apple juice, raw sugar, salt, mustard, soy sauce, and cayenne. With a fork or whisk, mix everything until well blended. Cover and refrigerate the mixture for up to 1 week.
7. In a small bowl, combine the salt, brown sugar, paprika, chili powder, granulated onion, granulated garlic, and pepper. Mix them well until fully blended. Store in an airtight container in a cool dry place for up to 2 months.

Turkey Bacon Dogs

Servings: 8
Cooking Time: 20 Minutes

Ingredients:
- 8 Nature's Own 100% Whole Wheat Hot Dog Rolls
- 1 package (16 ounces) Butterball Bun Size Premium Turkey Franks
- 8 slices Butterball Turkey Bacon
- 1/2 to 3/4 cup shredded Cheddar or Monterey Jack cheese
- Salsa (medium or hot)
- Pickled jalapeño pepper slices (optional)
- Sour cream (optional)

Directions:
1. Preheat the grill to 500°F using direct heat with a cast iron grate installed.
2. Spray cold grate of grill with cooking spray. Wrap each turkey frank with 1 slice turkey bacon. Grill franks, turning frequently, until bacon is crisp.
3. Place franks in hot dog rolls. Immediately sprinkle with cheese. Serve with salsa and if desired, jalapeno pepper slices and sour cream.

Pork Tortas Ahogada

Servings: 12
Cooking Time: 240 Minutes

Ingredients:
- 16 garlic cloves, minced
- 2 tbsp fresh oregano, minced
- 1/4 cup kosher salt, plus more as needed
- 1/4 ground black pepper, plus more as needed
- 9lb (4.1kg) boneless pork butt
- 12 hoagie buns
- for the sauce
- 6 tbsp vegetable oil
- 4 medium white onions, chopped
- 8 garlic cloves, minced
- 4 x 28oz (794g) cans whole peeled tomatoes
- 8 chipotle peppers in adobo
- 5 tsp dried oregano
- 1 1/2 tsp kosher salt
- 1/4 tsp sugar
- to smoke
- grapevine, peach, or oak wood chunks

Directions:

1. In a small bowl, combine garlic, oregano, salt, and pepper. Use a sharp knife to make 1-in (2.5-cm) cuts all over pork. Fill the cuts with the garlic mixture, and rub the exterior of the meat with more salt and pepper to taste.
2. Preheat the grill to 350°F (177°C). Once hot, add the wood chunks and install the heat deflector and a standard grate. Place pork in a shallow roasting pan (a disposable aluminum pan works well) and place the pan on the grate. Close the lid and roast until pork is tender, cooked through, and reaches an internal temperature of 190°F (88°C), about 2 to 3 hours. Remove pork from the grill and let rest for 20 minutes before slicing thinly, reserving the pan drippings.
3. To make the sauce, in a large pot on the stovetop over high heat, heat oil until almost smoking. Add onion and garlic, lower the heat to medium-high, and sauté until onion is translucent, about 2 to 3 minutes. Add the reserved pan drippings, tomatoes, peppers, oregano, salt, and sugar, and lower the heat to a simmer. Cook uncovered until the sauce is hot and the vegetables begin to soften, about 10 to 15 minutes, stirring frequently. Using an immersion blender, purée the sauce, then strain through a mesh sieve, using a spoon to press the liquid through.
4. Slice rolls in half lengthwise, removing some of the insides. Spoon 2 tbsp chipotle sauce over each half, top with the sliced pork, then spoon 1/4 cup sauce over each torta. Place tortas in a clean roasting pan and return to the grill until heated through, about 2 to 3 minutes. Serve immediately with any remaining sauce.

Sunday Dinner Pork Roast

Servings: 6
Cooking Time: 60 Minutes

Ingredients:

- 1 (3-4 lb) boneless pork loin roast
- 1/4 cup olive oil, separated
- 2 Tablespoons fresh thyme, chopped
- 2 Tablespoons Worcestershire sauce
- 1 Tablespoon soy sauce
- 4 cloves garlic, minced
- 2 lb small potatoes, halved (we like Yukon golds)
- 1 lb carrots, cut into 2 inch chunks
- 1 onion, cut into 2 inch chunks

Directions:

1. In a small bowl, combine Worcestershire sauce, soy sauce, thyme, garlic, and 2 Tablespoon olive oil.
2. Rinse and pat the pork loin dry.
3. In the bottom of a roasting pan, toss onion, potatoes and carrots with 2 Tablespoon olive oil, salt, and pepper.
4. Place the pork loin on top of the vegetables, fat side up and brush with the Worcestershire sauce mixture.
5. Grilling:
6. Preheat the grill to 425°F using direct heat with a cast iron grate installed.
7. Place the roasting pan on the grid and close the dome for 45 minutes to 1 hour or until the roast reaches an internal temperature of 150°F.
8. Allow the roast to rest for 10 minutes before slicing and serve with roasted vegetables on the side.

Sriracha Pork Chops

Servings:4
Cooking Time: 9 Minutes

Ingredients:
- 4 (1") boneless pork chops
- 2 Tablespoons Better Than Bouillon Reduced Sodium Roasted Chicken Base
- 1 Tablespoon minced garlic
- 1 Tablespoon Sriracha sauce
- 1 Tablespoon freshly chopped cilantro
- 1 Tablespoon freshly squeezed lime juice
- ¼ cup brown sugar
- 2 teaspoons freshly minced ginger

Directions:
1. Instructions Mix the Roasted Chicken Base, garlic, sriracha, cilantro, lime juice, brown sugar and ginger in a small mixing bowl. Add half of the mixture to a resealable plastic bag and add the pork chops and refrigerate for at least 3 hours and up to 8 hours.
2. Reserve the rest of the marinade, covered and refrigerated until ready to use.
3. Preheat the grill to 425°F using direct heat with a cast iron grate installed.
4. Remove the pork chops from the marinade and place directly onto the grill. Grill for 4 minutes. Using tongs, turn the pork chops and brush with the reserved marinade. Grill for an additional 4 – 5 minutes.
5. Remove the pork chops from the kamado grill and brush with the reserved marinade before serving.
6. Serve immediately.

Smoked Porchetta On The Grill

Servings: 12
Cooking Time: 370 Minutes

Ingredients:
- 1 pork belly
- 1 cup kosher salt
- 4 star anis, ground
- 10 black peppercorns, ground
- 5 allspice, ground
- 10 white peppercorns, ground
- 10 garlic cloves, smashed
- 3 sprigs thyme, chopped
- ½ cup granulated sugar
- 3 bunches broccoli raab
- 7 garlic cloves, shaved thin
- 1 tbsp butter
- 3 tsp red pepper flakes
- 1 tbsp lemon juice
- Salt and pepper to taste

Directions:
1. Twenty-four hours before your cook, mix all the aromatics together and rub into the pork belly on both sides. Cure the pork belly in a cooler.
2. Preheat the grill to 250°F using direct heat with a cast iron grate installed.
3. Rinse off the cure, then tie the pork belly into a roll with butcher twine. Place the rolled and tied pork belly in the grill. Smoke the belly until tender, around 4-6 hours or until an internal temperature reaches 165°F. Remove from the grill, untie and let rest for 10 minutes.
4. While the pork belly is resting, set up the kamado grill for direct cooking without the platesetter at 400°F.
5. Place the garlic and butter in a cast iron skillet. Cook garlic until it starts to brown then add the broccoli and the remaining ingredients. Cook the broccoli until it starts to wilt, roughly 5 minutes. Tip: add a touch of water if needed to help keep the pan from getting too hot. Remove from kamado grill and serve.
6. Slice the belly to desired thickness and serve with the braised broccoli raab.

Dr. Bbq's All Aces Baby Back Ribs

Servings: 9
Cooking Time: 60 Minutes

Ingredients:
- 3 slabs pork loin back ribs, about 6 pounds total
- 1 cup apple juice
- 1 cup   KC Style Sweet & Smoky Barbeque Sauce
- 1 cup   Vidalia Onion Sriracha Barbeque Sauce
- 1/4 cup raw sugar
- 3 tablespoons kosher salt
- 3 tablespoons paprika
- 2 tablespoons chili powder
- 1 teaspoon granulated onion
- 1 teaspoon granulated garlic
- 1 teaspoon cayenne

Directions:
1. Preheat the grill to 300°F using direct heat with a cast iron grate installed. Peel the membrane off the back of the ribs. Season the ribs liberally on all sides with Ray's Rub. Let the ribs rest for 10 minutes so the rub will get tacky, then place in a rib rack and cook for two hours.
2. Lay out three double sheets of heavy duty aluminum foil. Place a slab on each meaty side up. Fold up the edges and add 1/3 cup of apple juice to each packet. Put the ribs back on the kamado grill and cook for 1 hour or until tender when poked with a toothpick.
3. When the ribs are tender to your liking, remove from foil and return to kamado grill meaty side down. Combine the two sauces and mop/brush the ribs with a liberal coating. Cook for 15 minutes. Flip the ribs and brush the top of the ribs with sauce. Cook for 15 minutes. Brush with a second coat of sauce. Cook for 30 minutes until the sauce is set. Remove to a cutting board and cut each slab into 3 even pieces.
4. Add all ingredients in a bowl and mix.

Skewered Balinese Chicken

Servings: 8
Cooking Time: 10 Minutes

Ingredients:
- 10 garlic cloves, peeled
- 3 fresh cayenne peppers, halved and seeded
- 3 small shallots, halved
- 2 fresh bay leaves
- 1 tbsp chopped fresh ginger
- 1 tsp ground turmeric
- 4 tbsp vegetable oil, divided
- kosher salt and freshly ground black pepper
- 2lb (1kg) chicken breast, trimmed and cut into 1/2-in (1.25-cm) strips
- 4 limes, halved, to serve

Directions:
1. In a food processor, combine garlic, peppers, shallots, bay leaves, ginger, and turmeric. Pulse until finely chopped. Add 3 tbsp oil and pulse until the mixture forms a paste-like consistency.
2. In a sauté pan on the stovetop, heat remaining 1 tbsp oil over medium heat until shimmering. Add the spice paste, and cook until fragrant and lightly browned, about 5 minutes, stirring often. Remove the skillet from the heat, let the paste cool completely, and season with salt and pepper to taste.
3. Skewer the strips, place in a baking dish, and rub with the paste until thoroughly coated. Cover with plastic wrap and refrigerate for 4 hours or overnight.
4. Preheat the grill to 450°F (232°C) using direct heat with a cast iron grate installed. Place the chicken skewers on the grate, close the lid, and cook for 3 minutes per side. Transfer to a serving dish and squeeze lime juice over top before serving.

Perfect Ribs

Servings: 6
Cooking Time: 45 Minutes

Ingredients:
- 4 tbsp (60 ml) paprika
- 2 tbsp (30 ml) oregano
- 1 tbsp (15 ml) garlic powder
- 1 tbsp (15 ml) brown sugar
- 1 tbsp (15 ml) onion powder
- 1 tbsp (15 ml) dry mustard
- 2 tbsp (30 ml) cumin
- 2 tbsp (30 ml) salt

Directions:
1. Preheat the grill to 300°F using direct heat with a cast iron grate installed.
2. Combine all spices in a small bowl. Remove the membrane from the ribs and apply seasoning to both sides.
3. Place the ribs in the Rib and Roast Rack, bone side down, and cook for one hour. Flip the ribs and rotate the rack 180°. Cook for another hour.
4. Baste the ribs with the preserves (we used salted caramel peach preserves) then wrap tightly in foil – you do not want any gaps in the wrap or you will steam the ribs. Cook for an additional 30 minutes, then unwrap the ribs and place directly on the grid for a final 15 minutes to allow the glaze to tighten up.
5. Let rest for 5 to 10 minutes before serving.

Beer Brined Loin Chops

Servings: 6
Cooking Time: 15 Minutes

Ingredients:
- 6 boneless pork loin chops, cut 1 to 1 1/4 inch thick
- 2 cups water
- 2 cups ice
- 1/4 cup coarse salt
- 2 Tablespoons brown sugar
- 6 cloves garlic, minced
- 1 (12 oz) beer (we like Samuel Adams Cherry Wheat for its sweet and tart fruity flavor)

Directions:
1. In a small sauce pan, heat water, salt, and sugar together until salt and sugar are dissolved. Add cold beer, garlic, and ice.
2. Submerge pork chops into brine and allow to sit in the refrigerator for at least 2 hours and as long as overnight.
3. Remove the chops from the fridge and brine and pat dry.
4. Grilling:
5. Preheat the grill to 425°F using direct heat with a cast iron grate installed.
6. Place the pork chops on the grid and close the dome for 5 minutes.
7. Flip the pork chops and close the dome for another 5 minutes.
8. Close all vents and allow the pork to sit for another 3-5 minutes or until the internal temperature reaches 150°F.

FISH AND SEAFOOD

Tuna Kabobs

Servings: 2
Cooking Time: 10 Minutes

Ingredients:
- 2 tuna steaks, cut into 2-inch pieces
- 1 large red bell pepper, cut into 2-inch pieces
- 1 sweet onion, cut into 2-inch pieces
- 1 pineapple, cut into 2-inch pieces
- 1 cup Sweet Kentucky Bourbon Grilling Glaze
- Salt and pepper to taste

Directions:
1. Preheat the grill to 350°F using direct heat with a cast iron grate installed.
2. Thread the tuna, red bell peppers, onion and pineapple onto the skewers, leaving a small space between each item. Salt and pepper to taste.
3. Grill for 5 minutes then brush on the Sweet Kentucky Bourbon Grilling Glaze on both sides. Grill for another 5 minutes; glaze once more and remove from the kamado grill. Let rest for 10 minutes. Enjoy!

Justin Moore's Bbq Shrimp

Servings:2
Cooking Time: 10minutes

Ingredients:
- 1 pound peeled and deveined shrimp
- Cajun dry seasoning (I use Tony's)
- Good olive oil
- Fresh chopped garlic
- Freshly ground pepper
- Kosher salt
- Red pepper flakes

Directions:
1. Preheat the grill to 400°F using direct heat with a cast iron grate installed.
2. In a bowl, mix shrimp with all ingredients. Amounts of each depend on your taste … I like mine spicy, so I use a fair amount of Cajun spice and pepper flakes. Don't drown in olive oil, but make sure each shrimp is covered. Use skewers for cooking on the grill. Cook 3 to 4 minutes per side, then close all vents, and cook for 2 more minutes for a nice smoke flavor.
3. Serve over pasta, or as an appetizer with toasted French bread.

Scallops With Pea-sto

Servings: 4
Cooking Time: 7 Minutes

Ingredients:
- 1-lb sea scallops
- 2 Tablespoons olive oil
- Salt and Pepper
- Pea-sto
- 1 cup fresh green peas, blanched (you can also use frozen peas that have been thawed)
- 1/2 cup pecorino romano cheese, grated
- 1/4 cup basil leaves
- 1/4 cup mint leaves
- 3/4 tsp salt
- 1/2 tsp pepper
- 1/4 tsp crushed red chile flakes
- Olive oil

Directions:
1. In a food processor, combine peas, basil, mint, salt, pepper, and chile flakes and process until smooth. Add cheese.
2. Add enough olive oil until the pea-sto becomes a sauce-like consistency (about 1/2 cup). Set aside.
3. Grilling:
4. Preheat the grill to 400°F using direct heat with a cast iron grate installed.
5. Brush both sides of the scallops with olive oil and season with salt and pepper.
6. Place scallops on the grill and closer the dome for 3 minutes.
7. Gently flip the scallops and lower the dome for an additional 2-4 minutes.
8. Remove the scallops and pour some of the pea-sto on top.
9. Additional pea-sto can be saved in the fridge for 3 days. (It's delicious on pasta!)

Sesame Prawns

Servings: 4
Cooking Time: 10 Minutes

Ingredients:
- 1/4 cup (60 ml) coarsely chopped cilantro
- 2 tbsp (30 ml) chopped fresh mint leaves
- 2 scallions, coarsely chopped
- 1 tbsp (15 ml) chopped fresh ginger
- 2 garlic cloves
- 1/2 tsp (3 ml) red chili flakes (optional)
- 3 tbsp + 1/2 cup (165 ml) fat-free, low sodium chicken broth
- 1 tbsp (15 ml) canola or olive oil
- 1 cup (240 ml) coarsely chopped yellow onion
- 1 medium red bell pepper, diced
- 1 medium yellow bell pepper, diced
- 1 1/2 tsp (8 ml) toasted sesame oil
- 1 lb (450 g) prawns or jumbo shrimp, peeled and deveined
- 1/4 cup (60 ml) low-sodium soy sauce
- Salt and ground black pepper to taste
- 2 tsp (10 ml) toasted sesame seeds, for garnish
- 2 cups (480 ml) cooked wild or brown rice

Directions:
1. Combine the cilantro, mint, scallions, ginger, garlic, chili flakes and 3 tablespoons of the broth in a food processor. Pulse until the mixture is minced but not pureed. Set aside.
2. Preheat the grill to 400°F using direct heat with a cast iron grate installed.
3. In a Stir Fry & Paella Pan, heat the canola oil. Add the onion and bell peppers and cook for 5 minutes, or until the vegetables are just tender. Transfer to a bowl and cover with a towel to retain the heat.
4. Add the sesame oil to the pan. Add the cilantro mixture and cook for about 1 minute, stirring constantly. Add the remaining 1/2 cup to broth and bring to a boil. Add the prawns and soy sauce to the pan and cook for 2 minutes or until the prawns are just cooked. Return the onion/pepper mixture to the pan and stir for 1 minute to heat through.
5. Season with salt and black pepper. Garnish with toasted sesame seeds and serve with warm wild rice.

Grill-roasted Arctic Char

Servings: 4
Cooking Time: 27 Minutes

Ingredients:
- Butcher twine
- 2 leeks, trimmed, leaves separated and washed (16 leaves needed) 1 pear
- 1 sweet onion, thinly sliced into rings
- 1/2 cup (125 mL) fresh sage leaves
- Pinch of ground cinnamon
- Pinch of cayenne pepper
- Sea salt and freshly ground black pepper to taste
- 1 orange, halved
- 1 tbsp (15 mL) melted butter
- 2 arctic char fillets (approx. 8 oz/225 g each), skin on 4 to 5 slices bacon

Directions:

1. In a pot of boiling water, blanch the leek leaves for 1 minute or until tender and bright. Cool in ice water. Drain on paper towels.
2. Using a sharp knife, slice the pear into thin slices, cutting from the top of the pear to the bottom so that you get a cross-section of pear. Remove seeds. Place in a bowl. Add sliced onions and sage leaves and season with a little pinch of cinnamon, cayenne pepper, sea salt and black pepper. Squeeze the orange halves over top. Add melted butter and mix well. Set aside.
3. Using a sheet of plastic wrap a little longer than each of the fish fillets, lay 6 to 8 pieces of blanched leek onto the plastic, slightly overlapping. Place 1 fillet of arctic char, skin side down, crosswise across the middle of the leeks. Season the char fillet with a little salt and black pepper. Spread the stuffing mixture over the entire surface of the char.
4. Season the second fillet of arctic char with a little salt and black pepper. Lay fillet skin side up on the onion-pear stuffing. Starting on the edge closest to you, roll the leeks around the fish to make a tight leek wrap.
5. Next run your fingers along the top side of the bacon, pressing firmly to stretch the slice of bacon by about 25%. Wrap the bacon around the leek in three separate bands, leaving a swatch of leek in between. Cut 3 to 5 strips of butcher twine, each about 10 to 12 inches (25 to 30 cm) in length. Wrap one string around one strip of bacon and tie tightly around the fish bundle. Repeat with other strips of bacon and add a couple more if necessary. You don't want this bundle to fall apart. Cover and refrigerate to rest for 1 hour.
6. Preheat the grill to 400°F using direct heat with a cast iron grate installed.
7. Place the fish bundle onto the kamado grill directly over the heat. Grill for 10–12 minutes with the dome open, watching for flare-ups, until the bacon starts to crisp and you can see some juices come
8. from the fish. Using spatula, carefully turn fish over. Reduce grill heat and close dome. Continue to grill for another 10–15 minutes, until the bacon is crisp and the fish is just cooked through; ensure the stuffing is hot. Use a small metal skewer to test for doneness. Poke it in, and if it comes out hot, it's ready to go!
9. Remove from kamado grill. Remove butcher twine. Slice stuffed char into 2-inch (5 cm) thick slices. Serve immediately.

Seafood & Smoked Gouda Pasta

Servings: 12
Cooking Time: 40 Minutes

Ingredients:
- 1 red bell pepper, halved
- 4 asparagus stalks
- 8 tbsp olive oil
- 8 garlic cloves, minced
- 2lb (1kg) raw seafood, such as shrimp, scallops, or white fish, thawed if frozen
- kosher salt and freshly ground black pepper
- 16oz (450g) dried vermicelli
- crushed red pepper flakes, to garnish
- chopped fresh flat-leaf parsley, to garnish
- for the sauce
- 2 cups heavy cream
- 1/2 cup unsalted butter, softened
- 1/2 cup grated smoked gouda
- freshly ground black pepper

Directions:
1. Preheat the grill to 350°F (177°C) using direct heat with a cast iron grate installed and a dutch oven on the grate. Place pepper and asparagus on the grate (not in the dutch oven), close the grill lid, and grill until beginning to soften and char, about 7 to 10 minutes. Remove from the grill, chop, and set aside.
2. To the hot dutch oven, add olive oil and garlic. Cook until fragrant, about 30 seconds. Add seafood, season well with salt and pepper, and close the grill lid. Cook until seafood has begun to look opaque and take on color, about 5 minutes, stirring once. Transfer the cooked seafood to a cutting board and return the dutch oven to the grill. Cut seafood into bite-sized pieces. Set aside.
3. To make the sauce, add cream and butter to the hot dutch oven, and whisk gently until butter has melted. Sprinkle in smoked gouda, and stir to incorporate. Season with freshly ground black pepper to taste. Close the grill lid and reduce the cream sauce until just thickened, about 10 minutes, stirring occasionally.
4. On the stovetop, cook vermicelli according to package directions until cooked but still firm to the bite. Drain briefly in a colander.
5. Add seafood, pasta, and vegetables to the dutch oven. Gently toss to coat with the sauce. Garnish with crushed red pepper flakes and parsley. Serve immediately.

Thai Shrimp Skewers With Grilled Watermelon Salad

Servings: 4
Cooking Time: 10 Minutes

Ingredients:
- 1-lb U20 shrimp, peeled and deveined
- 4 wooden skewers, soaked in water for 30 minutes
- 1 cup Spicy Thai Marinade
- 1/4 cup olive oil
- 2 Tablespoon rice wine vinegar
- 1 tsp mint leaves, chopped
- 1 tsp fish sauce
- 1 round slice of watermelon, about 1 inch thick
- 1 English cucumber, diced
- 1 Fresno chile, sliced
- 1 shallot, finely diced

Directions:
1. Marinate the shrimp in the Spicy Thai Marinade for 20 minutes in the fridge.
2. In a large bowl, Fresno chile, shallot, vinegar, mint, fish sauce, and olive oil.
3. Grilling:
4. Preheat the grill to 400°F using direct heat with a cast iron grate installed.
5. Thread the shrimp onto the skewers and place on the grid. Close the dome for 3 minutes.
6. Flip the skewers and lower the dome for an additional 3 minutes or until the shrimp are opaque.
7. Brush the watermelon on both sides with olive oil and place on the grid for 30 seconds per side.
8. Dice watermelon and cucumber and stir into dressing.
9. Serve a scoop of the salad with a skewer of shrimp on top.

Greek Sea Bass

Servings: 4
Cooking Time: 15 Minutes

Ingredients:
- 2 whole sea bass (approximately 1 pound each), cleaned and gutted
- 1/4 cup olive oil
- 2 Tablespoons lemon juice
- 2 Tablespoons capers
- 2 Tablespoons parsley, chopped
- 1 tsp fresh oregano, chopped
- 1/2 tsp salt
- 1/4 tsp dried chili flakes
- 4 cloves garlic
- 1 lemon, thinly sliced

Directions:
1. Whisk together herbs, lemon juice, capers, olive oil, salt, and chili flakes. Set aside.
2. Season the sea bass with salt and pepper on the inside cavity and place lemon slices inside.
3. Grilling:
4. Preheat the grill to 400°F using direct heat with a cast iron grate installed.
5. Place whole fish on the grid and close the dome for 6 minutes.
6. Gently flip the fish and replace the dome for an additional 6-8 minutes or until the fish is cooked through.
7. Remove the sea bass and drizzle with herb and lemon mixture. Serve more on the side for dressing as the fish is eaten.

Cedar Planked Jerk Coconut Shrimp

Servings: 4
Cooking Time: 12 Minutes

Ingredients:
- 8 large shrimp, shell on and deveined if available
- 2 tbsp unsweetened shredded Coconut
- 2 tbsp Jamaican Jerk seasoning
- 2 green onions, sliced
- Cedar Grilling Planks

Directions:
1. Preheat the grill to 425°F using direct heat with a cast iron grate installed. Soak the plank in hot water for at least 15 minutes.
2. Toss the shrimp in the jerk seasoning and arrange them on the planks. Sprinkle the coconut on top of the shrimp. Set the loaded planks on the kamado grill and cook for 8-12 minutes or until the shrimp are pink and firm.
3. Remove from the grill and top with sliced green onion. Serve immediately.

Shrimp & Cheddar Tostada

Servings: 6
Cooking Time: 10 Minutes

Ingredients:
- ¼ cup fat free cream cheese, softened
- ¼ cup reduced-fat mayonnaise
- 2 tablespoons skim milk
- ¼ cup finely chopped fresh cilantro
- 2 tablespoons fresh lime juice, divided
- 30 medium-size shrimp, peeled and deveined (about 1 pound)
- 2 tablespoons barbecue rub or seasoning
- ½ teaspoon salt
- Cooking spray
- 6 (6-inch) corn tortillas
- 4 ounces Cabot Jalapeno Light Cheddar or Cabot Sharp Light Cheddar, grated (about 1 cup)
- 6 tablespoons finely chopped fresh tomato

Directions:
1. In small bowl, combine cream cheese, mayonnaise and milk; whisk until smooth. Stir in cilantro and 1 tablespoon of lime juice. Cover and refrigerate until serving time.
2. When ready to serve, thread 5 shrimp onto flexible skewers. In small bowl, combine barbecue rub and salt. Brush shrimp with remaining 1 tablespoon lime juice and dredge in rub mixture. Place kabobs in shallow dish; cover and refrigerate for 15 minutes.
3. Preheat the grill to 350°F using direct heat with a cast iron grate installed.
4. Place kabobs on kamado grill grid coated with cooking spray and cook for 3 minutes on each side, or until done. Set aside.
5. Place tortillas directly on kamado grill and cook for 4 minutes. Top each tortilla with some of cheese and bake until cheese is melted, about 3 minutes longer.
6. Place 1 tortilla on each of 6 individual serving plates. Top each with 5 grilled shrimp and 2 tablespoons cilantro mayonnaise. Sprinkle with tomato and serve.

Bacon-wrapped Stuffed Shrimp

Servings: 4
Cooking Time: 20 Minutes

Ingredients:
- 4 jumbo shrimp
- ¼ cup fresh crab meat
- 1 teaspoon olive oil
- ¼ teaspoon black pepper
- ¼ teaspoon red pepper
- ¼ teaspoon salt
- ¼ teaspoon parsley
- ¼ teaspoon lemon juice, fresh
- 4 slices of bacon
- 1 cup Italian dressing

Directions:
1. Preheat the grill to 350°F using direct heat with a cast iron grate installed.
2. Devein and butterfly the shrimp. Place the shrimp and Italian dressing in a freezer bag and marinate for at least 2 hours.
3. In a skillet, sauté the fresh crabmeat with olive oil, salt, black pepper, red pepper, parsley and lemon juice. Place a spoonful of the crabmeat in the shrimp and lay on the end of the bacon. Roll up the shrimp and bacon and fold it over to ensure crab meat stays intact. Place the shrimp on the Grid. Sear the bacon for a few minutes on each side. Cook for 20 minutes or until shrimp is pink.

Ricky Taylor's Peri Peri Lobster

Servings: 4
Cooking Time: 10 Minutes

Ingredients:
- 4 medium lobster tails
- Juice of 3 lemons
- 1 clove of garlic, minced
- 1 tbsp olive oil
- 3 tbsp salted butter
- ½ tsp Peri Peri powder
- ½ tsp salt
- 1 tsp white wine vinegar
- 2-3 cups cooked white rice

Directions:
1. Preheat the grill to 375°F using direct heat with a cast iron grate installed.
2. For the Peri Peri sauce: Oil a Stir-Fry and Paella Pan with the olive oil; place on the grid and add garlic. Stir the garlic for 1-2 minutes. Add the lemon juice until hot but not boiling. Add the butter, Peri Peri, salt and the white wine vinegar (½ tsp of Peri Peri is quite spicy, adjust that amount to taste).
3. For the lobster: Clean and butterfly the lobster tails, baste with ¼ of the sauce.
4. Place the lobster on the kamado grill meat side down for 8 minutes, basting throughout.
5. Remove the lobsters from the shells and serve over rice; drizzle with remaining Peri Peri sauce.

Savory Pecan Shrimp Scampi Over Spaghetti Squash

Servings: 6

Cooking Time: 50 Minutes

Ingredients:
- 1¼ lbs. large shrimp, peeled and deveined
- 2 tbsp   Savory Pecan Seasoning
- 3 tbsp olive oil, divided plus more to coat the pans
- 1 (2-3 pounds) spaghetti squash
- 2 tablespoons unsalted butter
- 3 cloves garlic, minced
- 1 shallot, minced
- ¼ cup dry white wine
- ½ cup fresh basil leaves
- 1 tbsp freshly squeezed lemon juice
- 2 tbsp freshly grated Parmesan
- Kosher salt and freshly ground black pepper, to taste

Directions:
1. Preheat the grill to 375°F using direct heat with a cast iron grate installed.
2. Coat the shrimp with 1 tablespoon extra-virgin olive oil and Savory Pecan Seasoning; then thread them onto the bamboo skewers.
3. Grease the roasting pan with a thin layer of extra virgin olive oil. Cut the squash into 1½ inch rounds; coat with 2 tablespoons extra virgin olive oil and season with salt. Place the squash rounds into the roasting pan, and place on the indirect side of the kamado grill. Roast until tender, about 35-45 minutes. Remove from the kamado grill, and let rest for 10 minutes.
4. Place the Cast Iron Skillet on the indirect side to preheat. Melt butter and a drizzle of olive oil; add garlic and shallots. Cook, stirring occasionally. Add the white wine and let the mixture cook down about 25%.
5. Using a fork, shred the fleshy part of the squash into strands. Add the squash the skillet. Cook, stirring occasionally, until the squash is heated through, about 2-3 minutes. Chiffonade the basil, then add the basil and lemon juice to the skillet; season with salt and pepper to taste.
6. While the skillet mixture is heating, grill the shrimp for 2 minutes on each side on the direct side of the spander. Add the squash "noodles" to a bowl. Serve immediately, topped with shrimp and Parmesan.

Grilled Shrimp

Servings: 4
Cooking Time: 18 Minutes

Ingredients:
- 1 lb shrimp, 16/20 size, peeled and deveined
- ¼ cup olive oil
- ¼ cup lemon juice
- 3 tbsp fresh chopped parsley
- Coarse salt and freshly cracked pepper
- 1 cup dry white wine
- 1 cup shallots minced
- ½ cup unsalted butter, cut into ½ inch cubes, chilled
- 1 tbsp   Citrus & Dill Sauce Seasoning
- 1 tbsp fresh lemon juice

Directions:
1. Preheat the grill to 450°F using direct heat with a cast iron grate installed.
2. In a large, non-reactive bowl, stir together the olive oil, lemon juice, parsley, salt and black pepper. Add shrimp and toss to coat. Marinate in the refrigerator for 30 minutes.
3. For the sauce: In a small saucepan, heat the wine and shallots over medium-high heat until reduced to 2 tablespoons, about 12-15 minutes. Turn off the heat and gradually add each cube of butter into the reduction, whisking after each
4. addition. Add the Citrus & Dill Seasoning, and season with salt as desired. Whisk in the lemon juice and set sauce aside.
5. Place the shrimp on a lightly oiled Perforated Cooking Grid and cook for 2 to 3 minutes per side, or until opaque. Serve the shrimp drizzled with the sauce over quinoa or rice.

Southern Catfish

Servings: 6
Cooking Time: 30 Minutes

Ingredients:
- 3 medium tomatoes chopped
- ¼ cup chopped onion
- 2 jalapeno peppers, seeded and finely chopped
- 2 Tablespoons white wine vinegar
- 3 teaspoons salt, divided
- 3 teaspoons paprika
- 3 teaspoons chili powder
- 1 ½ teaspoons ground cumin
- 1 – 1 ½ teaspoons ground coriander
- ¾ -1 teaspoons cayenne pepper
- ½ teaspoon garlic powder
- 4 catfish fillets

Directions:
1. Combine tomatoes, onion, jalapenos, vinegar and 1-teaspoon salt. Cover and refrigerate for at least 30 minutes.
2. Combine paprika, chili powder, cumin, coriander, cayenne, garlic powder and remaining salt; rub over fish.
3. Preheat the grill to 350°F using direct heat with a cast iron grate installed.
4. Gill fillets on Perforated Cooking Grid.
5. Serve with your favorite salsa.

DESSERTS

Best Banana Bread

Servings: 6
Cooking Time: 40 Minutes

Ingredients:
- 1 cup plain yogurt
- 1/4 cup butter
- 3 very ripe bananas, peeled
- 2 eggs
- 2 cups flour
- 2/3 cups sugar
- 3/4 tsp salt
- 1/2 tsp vanilla extract
- 1/2 tsp baking soda
- 1/4 tsp baking powder

Directions:
1. In a blender, combine bananas, yogurt, sugar, butter, vanilla, and eggs until smooth.
2. In a large bowl, sift together flour, salt, baking powder, and baking soda.
3. Gradually add the wet ingredients into the dry ingredients and gently stir to combine. DO NOT OVER MIX.
4. Line a dutch oven with a liner.
5. Pour batter into the dutch oven and cover.
6. Grilling:
7. Preheat the grill to 350°F using direct heat with a cast iron grate installed and place the dutch oven on the grid.
8. Lower the dome for 30 minutes or until a toothpick inserted into the center comes out clean.

Grilled Sopapillas

Servings: 6
Cooking Time: 18 Minutes

Ingredients:
- 1 pizza dough, divided into 6 pieces
- 3 Tablespoons melted butter
- 1/4 cup sugar
- 1 Tablespoon cinnamon

Directions:
1. Stretch dough into round shape.
2. Place the dough directly on the pizza stone in a 500°F grill.
3. Brush with melted butter and top with cinnamon sugar.
4. Close the dome for 3 minutes, then remove.
5. Repeat with remaining dough.

Grilled Fruit Pie

Servings: 8
Cooking Time: 55 Minutes

Ingredients:
- for the crust
- 1 cup all-purpose flour, plus extra for rolling dough
- 1/2 tsp kosher salt
- 1/2 cup butter, chilled and cut into small cubes
- 1/4 cup ice water
- 2lb (1kg) dried beans, for blind baking
- powdered sugar, for dusting
- whipped cream or ice cream, to serve (optional)
- for the filling
- 1 1/4lb (565g) seasonal fruit, such as pears and plums, halved and pitted
- 1/2 cup sugar
- 4 tbsp cornstarch
- 2 tbsp lemon juice

Directions:
1. Preheat the grill to 350°F (177°C) using indirect heat with a standard grate installed. Place fruit on the grate skin side up, keeping them toward the edges of the grate. Close the lid and grill until beginning to soften, about 3 to 5 minutes. Transfer to a cutting board and slice. Set aside.
2. To make the crust, in a food processor, combine flour and salt, pulsing 3 to 4 times. Add butter, and pulse until the texture is mealy, about 5 to 6 times. With the food processor running, slowly add the ice water in 1 tbsp increments until the dough comes together.
3. Turn out the dough onto a floured work surface and sprinkle with flour. Using a rolling pin, roll dough out to a 10- to 11-in (25- to 28-cm) circle. Carefully transfer the dough to a 9-in (23-cm) metal pie pan, pressing the dough to the edges. Trim any overhang and crimp the edges. Prick the dough with a fork to prevent bubbles during baking. Place the pan in the fridge to chill for 15 minutes.
4. Spread a large piece of parchment paper over the dough and fill the pan with dry beans, pressing them into the edges of the dough. Place the pan on the grate, close the lid, and bake for 10 minutes. Remove the parchment and beans from the pan, and continue baking the crust until golden brown in color, about 10 to 15 minutes more. Remove the pan from the grill and let the crust cool completely before filling.
5. To make the filling, in a large bowl, combine sugar, cornstarch, and juice. Add the grilled fruit and toss lightly to coat. Pour the fruit mixture into the baked crust. Place on the grate, close the lid, and bake until the filling is thickened and bubbling at the edges, about 30 minutes.
6. Remove the pie from the grill and place on a wire rack to cool. Just before serving, sprinkle with powdered sugar. Serve with whipped cream or ice cream (if desired).

Apple Cake

Servings: 12
Cooking Time: 60 Minutes

Ingredients:
- 2 (21 oz) cans apple pie filling
- 1 (14 oz) jar caramel ice cream topping
- 1 box yellow cake mix, prepared according to package directions and mixed with 2 tsp cinnamon

Directions:
1. Prepare cake according to package directions.
2. Line a dutch oven with a liner.
3. Pour pie filling into the bottom of the dutch oven.
4. Top with caramel ice cream topping.
5. Top with prepared cake mix.
6. Grilling:
7. Preheat the grill to 350°F using direct heat with a cast iron grate installed.
8. Cover the dutch oven and place on the grid of the grill.
9. Lower the dome and cook for 1 hour.
10. Serve warm with whipped cream or ice cream.

Upside Down Triple Berry Pie

Servings: 8
Cooking Time: 35 Minutes

Ingredients:
- 6 cups frozen triple berry mix
- 2 Tablespoons lemon juice
- 1 refrigerated pie crust
- 1 cup sugar, divided
- 4 Tablespoons cornstarch

Directions:
1. Place a liner in the dutch oven.
2. In a separate bowl, combine frozen berries with 3/4 cup sugar, cornstarch, and lemon juice.
3. Pour berries into the bottom of the lined dutch oven.
4. Unroll pie crust and place on top of berry mixture.
5. Cut 4 vent holes into the crust.
6. Sprinkle remaining sugar over the pie crust.
7. Grilling:
8. Preheat the grill to 425°F using direct heat with a cast iron grate installed.
9. Cover the dutch oven and place on the grid.
10. Lower the dome for 35 minutes or until the crust is golden and the berry mixture has thickened.
11. Cut the crust as you would any pie.
12. Serve a piece of crust topped with ice cream and a scoop of the thickened berry mixture.

S'mores Pizza

Servings: 8
Cooking Time: 5 Minutes

Ingredients:
- 1 pizza dough
- 1/2 cup semi-sweet chocolate chips
- 1/2 cup miniature marshmallows
- 1/4 cup slightly crushed graham crackers

Directions:
1. Stretch dough to a 14" round and place on a pizza peel.
2. Sprinkle dough with chocolate chips, miniature marshmallows, and graham cracker crumbs.
3. Grilling:
4. Slide the pizza onto the prepared stone at 500°F.
5. Cook for 5 minutes, remove from the stone, slice, and serve.

Lemon Poppy Seed Cake

Servings: 10
Cooking Time: 45 Minutes

Ingredients:
- 1 tsp poppy seeds
- 2 lemons, zested and juiced
- 1 vanilla cake mix prepared according to package directions, substituting melted butter for oil and buttermilk for water
- 1 lb powdered sugar
- 4 ounces cream cheese
- 1 stick butter, softened
- 1/2 tsp vanilla
- 1/2 tsp lemon extract
- The juice and zest of 1 lemon

Directions:
1. Prepare cake mix according to package directions, substituting melted butter for the oil and buttermilk for the water.
2. Add the lemon zest, lemon juice, and poppy seeds.
3. Line the dutch oven with a liner.
4. Pour prepare cake mix into the liner and cover.
5. Grilling:
6. Preheat the grill to 350°F using direct heat with a cast iron grate installed.
7. Place the dutch oven on the grid and lower the dome for 30-40 minutes or until a toothpick inserted into the center comes out clean.
8. Meanwhile, combine glaze ingredients, adding milk to thin out the glaze if necessary.
9. Remove the cake from the grill and set aside to cool for 10 minutes before pouring glaze over the cake.
10. Serve warm.

Seasonal Fruit Cobbler

Servings: 12
Cooking Time: 90 Minutes

Ingredients:
- 2lb (1kg) seasonal fruit, washed, pitted (if needed), and sliced or halved if needed
- 1/2 tsp ground cinnamon
- 2 tsp cornstarch (for juicy fruits; omit for pears or apples)
- 4 tbsp butter, plus more for greasing
- 1/2 cup sugar, plus more for sprinkling
- 3/4 cup self-rising flour
- 3/4 cup whole milk
- whipped cream, to serve

Directions:
1. Preheat the grill to 350°F (177°C) using indirect heat with a standard grate installed. Place the fruit on the grate (or in a cast iron skillet if the fruit might fall through the grate), close the lid, and grill until beginning to soften and char, about 7 to 10 minutes. Remove fruit from the grill and place in a large bowl. Sprinkle cinnamon and cornstarch (if using) over fruit, and add a little sugar (if desired). Gently toss to coat and set aside.
2. Grease a 9-in (23-cm) grill-safe baking pan with butter. On the stovetop in a small saucepan, heat 4 tbsp butter over medium-low heat until beginning to brown, about 10 to 15 minutes.
3. In a medium bowl, whisk together butter, sugar, flour, and milk. Transfer fruit to the prepared baking pan and spread the batter evenly over top. Place the pan on the grate, close the lid, and bake until golden brown and bubbly, about 1 hour. In the last 10 minutes of cooking, sprinkle a light amount of sugar over top. Remove the cobbler from the grill, and serve warm with whipped cream on top.

Pizza Margherita

Servings: 2
Cooking Time: 6 Minutes

Ingredients:
- cornmeal, for dusting
- 1/4 cup marinara sauce
- 2oz (55g) fresh mozzarella, sliced
- 3 garlic cloves, thinly sliced
- 12–16 fresh basil leaves
- kosher salt and freshly ground black pepper
- grated Parmesan, to serve
- for the dough
- 12oz (340g) Italian 00 flour, plus more for dusting
- 4 tsp kosher salt
- 2 tsp instant dry yeast
- 6 1/2oz (190ml) warm water (105°F [41°C])

Directions:
1. To make the dough, in a large bowl, whisk together flour, salt, and yeast until well combined. Add water, and use your hands to mix until no dry flour remains. Cover tightly with plastic wrap and allow to rise at room temperature for 2 to 4 hours. Turn the dough out onto a lightly floured surface and allow to sit at room temperature for 2 hours before baking.
2. Preheat the grill to 600°F (316°C) using indirect heat with a pizza stone resting directly on the heat deflector. (The pizza stone should be level with the grill rim.)
3. On a lightly floured work surface, roll out the dough to 1/4 in (.5cm) thick and a 10-in (25cm) diameter. Lightly dust a pizza paddle or unrimmed baking sheet with cornmeal, and place the dough on top. Evenly spread the sauce over the dough, working from the center to the edges. Top with the sliced mozzarella and garlic.
4. Carefully slide the pizza from the paddle to the hot pizza stone. Close the lid and bake until the crust is golden brown and the cheese is melted and beginning to bubble, about 4 to 6 minutes.
5. Use the pizza paddle to remove the pizza from the grill. Scatter the basil leaves over top and sprinkle with salt, pepper, and Parmesan.

Peach Dutch Baby

Servings: 8
Cooking Time: 25 Minutes

Ingredients:
- 8 oz frozen peaches, thawed (or 3 ripe peaches, peeled and sliced)
- 1 cup whole milk
- 4 eggs
- 1 cup flour
- 1/4 cup sugar
- 1/4 cup butter
- 1 tsp vanilla
- 1 tsp cinnamon
- 1/2 tsp salt

Directions:
1. In a blender, combine milk, flour, sugar, vanilla, cinnamon, salt, and eggs until smooth.
2. Grilling:
3. Preheat the grill to 425°F using direct heat with a cast iron grate installed.
4. Place the dutch oven on the grid of the grill and melt the butter.
5. Line the bottom of the pot with peaches and pour over milk and egg mixture.
6. Close the dome for 20 minutes or until the top of the Dutch Baby is golden brown.
7. Serve with a sprinkling of powdered sugar.

Caramel Cinnamon Rolls

Servings: 4
Cooking Time: 30 Minutes

Ingredients:
- 18 frozen cinnamon rolls, thawed (you can also used canned cinnamon rolls)
- 1/2 cup brown sugar
- 1/2 cup graham cracker crumbs
- 1/2 cup caramel ice cream topping
- 1 tsp cinnamon

Directions:
1. Line the dutch oven with a liner.
2. Cut each cinnamon roll into 4 pieces and arrange them around the bottom of the dutch oven.
3. In a separate bowl, combine brown sugar, graham cracker crumbs, and cinnamon.
4. Sprinkle some of the mixture over the layer of cinnamon rolls. Repeat.
5. Grilling:
6. Preheat the grill to 350°F using direct heat with a cast iron grate installed.
7. Cover the dutch oven and place it on the grid of the grill.
8. Lower the dome for 25-30 minutes or until the cinnamon rolls are golden brown.
9. Drizzle caramel ice cream topping over the warm rolls and serve.

Nutella And Strawberry Pizza

Servings: 8
Cooking Time: 5 Minutes

Ingredients:
- 1 pizza dough
- 1/2 lb sliced strawberries
- 1/4 cup Nutella

Directions:
1. Stretch the pizza dough into a 14 inch round and place it on a pizza peel.
2. Spread the dough with the Nutella and top with strawberries.
3. Grilling:
4. Slide the pizza onto the prepared stone in a 500°F grill and cook for 5 minutes.
5. Remove from the stone with a pizza peel and slice into 8 pieces.

Grilled Naan

Servings: 24
Cooking Time: 6 Minutes

Ingredients:
- 1 cup warm water (105°F [41°C])
- 1/4oz (7g) active dry yeast
- 1/4 cup sugar
- 3 tbsp whole milk
- 1 large egg, beaten
- 2 tsp kosher salt
- 20 1/4oz (575g) bread flour, plus more for kneading
- vegetable oil, for greasing
- 1/4 cup butter, melted

Directions:
1. In a large bowl, combine water and yeast. Let sit until frothy, about 10 minutes. Stir in sugar, milk, egg, salt, and flour to make a soft dough. Knead on a lightly floured surface until smooth.
2. Lightly oil a large bowl, place the dough in the bowl, and cover with a damp cloth. Let sit to rise until the dough has doubled in volume, about 1 hour.
3. Punch the dough down and divide it into 4 balls (about the size of golf balls). Cover with a towel and allow to rise until the balls have doubled in size, about 30 minutes.
4. Preheat the grill to 425°F (218°C) using direct heat with a cast iron grate installed. Use a rolling pin one ball of dough into a thin circle. Lightly oil the grate, place the circle of dough on the grate, close the lid, and bake until puffy and lightly browned, about 2 to 3 minutes. Brush the uncooked side with butter, then flip the dough over and brush the cooked side with butter. Cook until puffy and lightly browned, about 3 minutes more. Repeat the cooking process with the remaining dough. (You can also bake all 4 balls at the same time.)
5. Remove the naan from the grill and sprinkle with seasoning of choice (if desired). Serve warm.

Buttermilk Biscuits

Servings: 6
Cooking Time: 15 Minutes

Ingredients:
- 3/4 cups buttermilk
- 1/2 cup butter, cut into 1/2 inch cubes
- 3 cups flour
- 1 1/2 tsp baking powder
- 1/2 tsp salt

Directions:
1. In the bowl of a food processor, combine flour, baking powder, salt and butter and pulse until the butter is the size of small peas.
2. With the food processor going, stream in buttermilk until the dough just comes together.
3. Turn out on a floured surface.
4. Pat the dough to 1/2-inch thickness and fold in half.
5. Pat the dough to 1/2-inch thickness and fold in half again.
6. Pat the dough a third time to 1/2-inch thickness.
7. Using a pizza cutter, cut the dough into 12 square biscuits.
8. Place a sheet of parchment in the bottom of the dutch oven.
9. Place biscuits on the bottom of the dutch oven, being careful that they do not touch. (You may have to do this in two batches.)
10. Grilling:
11. Preheat the grill to 425°F using direct heat with a cast iron grate installed.
12. Cover the dutch oven with the lid and place on the grid.
13. Lower the dome for 12-15 minutes.
14. Biscuits are done when they are golden brown. Serve with butter, honey, or jam.

Bread Pudding

Servings: 8
Cooking Time: 60 Minutes

Ingredients:
- 1 1/2 cups milk
- 10 eggs
- 1 loaf French bread, cut into 1 1/2 inch cubes
- 1 1/2 cups sugar
- 1 cup raisins (optional)
- 2 Tablespoons vanilla
- 2 tsp cinnamon
- 1/2 tsp nutmeg
- 1/4 tsp salt

Directions:
1. Line the dutch oven with a liner.
2. Place bread cubes and raisins into the dutch oven.
3. In a large bowl, combine eggs, milk, sugar, vanilla, cinnamon, nutmeg, and salt.
4. Pour the mixture over the bread and raisins.
5. Allow the bread mixture to sit for 30 minutes.
6. Grilling:
7. Preheat the grill to 350°F using direct heat with a cast iron grate installed.
8. Cover the dutch oven, place it on the grid, and lower the dome for 1 hour.
9. Serve the bread pudding with vanilla ice cream or whipped cream.

RECIPES INDEX

A

Asian Flank Steak 9

Apple Cake 106

B

Baby Back Ribs With Guava Barbecue Sauce 72

Bacon Wrapped Jalapeño Stuffed Chicken Thighs 58

Bacon-wrapped Bbq Quail 57

Bacon-wrapped Stuffed Shrimp 97

Barbecue Chicken With Alabama White Sauce 63

Beer Brined Loin Chops 85

Beer Can Bbq Burgers 20

Best Banana Bread 102

Bread Pudding 117

Breakfast Burger 48

Buffa-que Wings 53

Burnt End Baked Beans 32

Buttermilk Biscuits 116

C

Caramel Cinnamon Rolls 113

Cedar Planked Jerk Coconut Shrimp 95

Cheesy Tomato Risotto 41

Chicken Keema Burgers 61

Chutney-glazed Brisket 26

Classic American Burger 45

Corn & Tomato Salsa 36

Corn, Bacon & Chorizo Hash 37

Cuban Chicken Bombs 60

D

Dr. Bbq's All Aces Baby Back Ribs 82

Dr. Bbq's Spare Rib Surprise 74

Dry Rub Smoked Chicken Wings With Buttermilk "berliner Weisse" Ranch 55

Dutch Oven Baked Beans 29

G

Greek Sea Bass 94

Green Chile Chicken Chili 50

Grilled Endive Salad 30

Grilled Entrecôte Of Beef 14

Grilled Fruit Pie 104

Grilled Lemon Garlic Zucchini 35

Grilled Naan 115

Grilled Onions 34

Grilled Shrimp 100

Grilled Sopapillas 103

Grilled Vegetable & Couscous Salad 39

Grill-roasted Arctic Char 90

H
Ham & Cheese Panini 68
Hoisin Grilled Rabbit 12

J
Jalapeño Brisket Flat 22
Justin Moore's Bbq Shrimp 87

L
Lemon Pepper Wings 59
Lemon Poppy Seed Cake 109

M
Maple Brined Pork Chops 67
Moppin' Sauce-marinated Flank Steak Fajitas 28

N
Nutella And Strawberry Pizza 114

O
Oahu Burger 44
Open-faced Leftover Turkey Sandwich 51

P
Peach Dutch Baby 112
Perfect Ribs 84
Pizza Margherita 111
Planked Bison Sliders 10
Pork Curry 70

Pork Tortas Ahogada 77
Potato, Squash, And Tomato Gratin 31
Prime Rib Roast 21

Q
Quesadilla Burger 46

R
Ratatouille 40
Reverse Seared Ribeyes 25
Ricky Taylor's Peri Peri Lobster 98
Rosemary Ranch Chicken Kebabs 49
Rotisserie Chicken 62

S
S'mores Pizza 108
Savory Beer Can Chicken 66
Savory Pecan Shrimp Scampi Over Spaghetti Squash 99
Scallops With Pea-sto 88
Seafood & Smoked Gouda Pasta 92
Seared Bison Filet 17
Seasonal Fruit Cobbler 110
Sesame Prawns 89
Shrimp & Cheddar Tostada 96
Skewered Balinese Chicken 83
Smoked Beef Short Ribs 18
Smoked Ham On Grill 69
Smoked Porchetta On The Grill 81
Smoked Potato Salad 43

Southern Catfish 101

Spicy Lamb Skewers (yang Rou Chuan) 24

Sriracha Pork Chops 80

Steak & Egg Sandwich 16

Stuffed Caprese Chicken Sandwich 65

Summer Squash & Eggplant 38

Sunday Dinner Pork Roast 79

T

Tex Mex Burger 23

Thai Shrimp Skewers With Grilled Watermelon Salad 93

The Crowned Jewels Burger 47

Tuna Kabobs 86

Turkey Bacon Dogs 76

U

Ultimate Chicken Curry 52

Upside Down Triple Berry Pie 107

W

Wood-plank Loaded Mashed Potatoes 42

Wood-plank Stuffed Tomatoes 33

Lightning Source UK Ltd.
Milton Keynes UK
UKHW032053250822
407860UK00005BA/217